Behind ——— The Headlines

*How a
Conservative
Beauty Queen
Became a Target
of Fake News and
Cancel Culture*

Behind The Headlines

*How a
Conservative
Beauty Queen
Became a Target
of Fake News and
Cancel Culture*

KARYN TURK

Post Hill
PRESS

A POST HILL PRESS BOOK
ISBN: 978-1-63758-008-0
ISBN (eBook): 978-1-63758-009-7

Behind the Headlines:
How a Conservative Beauty Queen Became a Target
of Fake News and Cancel Culture

Cover Photo Credit: Stevan Fane
FaneFoto.com

Post Hill Press
New York • Nashville
posthillpress.com

Published in the United States of America
1 2 3 4 5 6 7 8 9 10

In loving memory of Ilse & Joe

Contents

Foreword by Roger Stone

Karyn Turk is most definitely not a Karen. Deeply suspicious of big government, and with enough experience with the elites of society who, unlike the rest of us, are not subject to the laws and regulations that are enforced for the masses, Karyn is a tireless advocate for freedom with seemingly unlimited energy. In fact, Karyn has been in the frontline of the effort to "Make America Great Again" since its inception.

Always stylish, and rarely found at a cocktail party without a drink in her hand, wearing the most chic shoes, and the perfect dress, Karyn is literally the apostle of pep. Always shuffling between podcasts, radio shows, and television. She keeps a schedule that would exhaust a twenty-two year old, Karyn is committed to exposing a narrative far different than the one the government seeks to sell the American people every day.

There are those who criticize Karyn because of what they view as her excess self-promotion. This reminds me of one of *Stone's Rules*: *"If you don't promote yourself, who will promote you?!"* Karyn Turk is canny enough to know that she has to have a brand before she can effectively sell a message of freedom and skepticism of a government so obviously missing from the marketplace of ideas today.

Much like me, Karyn has had her own brush with the U.S. Department of Justice and was prosecuted for "crimes" that normally would not undergo either detection or prosecution were she not an extraordinarily prominent supporter of President Donald J. Trump. Karyn faced her fate with bravery and dignity and emerged with her spirit undaunted and her tenacity unimpeded. The entire experience might have destroyed a lesser woman. Karyn Turk is a warrior, she is also a survivor.

I have noticed in her an ability to separate those who will actually do what they say they will do from the epic number of bullshitters who seem to pervade any viable political enterprise.

If Karyn Turk was a man, she'd be what the late Roy Cohn called "a stand up guy." Always cheerful, never discouraged, and always on the move, Karyn Turk is a human dynamo and a one woman truth squad. Her book will infuse you with the same energy. Enjoy.

Chapter 1 ———————————

The Surrender

𝕴n 2019, there were a lot of headlines about me; if you didn't read them back then, you were in the minority. The clickbait spread like a virus before Covid was a thing. Once the first story hit the internet, the others reproduced like rabbits, and each time, the narrative went to a new low.

The Palm Beach Post kicked it off: "Conservative commentator Karyn Turk admits to stealing mom's Social Security. Fresh from hosting a fundraiser for the legal defense of Republican operative Roger Stone, conservative media commentator Karyn Turk on Friday admitted she stole her 83-year-old mother's Social Security checks."

Other outlets ran with this information, and the headlines grew more sensational with each publication. Obviously, they used a political angle—why wouldn't they in the divided climate of 2019? They made me appear as if I was taking checks out of a little old lady's purse and wouldn't stop. I was a monstrous thief.

It was always a relentless onslaught of attacks mixed with political undertones. "Looking relaxed and unperturbed," *The Post* wrote, "Karyn Turk pleads guilty in U.S. District Court to a single charge of Social Security fraud. Because the charge is a misdemeanor, the 47-year-old Highland Beach woman who uses social media and her radio and television shows to defend all things Republican would not lose her ability to vote - a right she described as 'very important to me.' Instead of using $17,300 in government checks to pay for the care of her mother, who was ravaged by dementia, Turk used the money for herself, said Assistant U.S. Attorney Adrienne Rabinowitz. Turk didn't dispute the prosecutor's description of her crime. While she and her attorney, Guy Fronstin, declined comment as they left the courthouse, both said additional information would surface that would explain her actions. The criminal charges stemmed from an ugly fight in probate court that began when she didn't pay for her mother's expenses at the American Finnish Nursing Home in Lake Worth, records show."

There were shreds of truth in this fake news. It was true that I held a fundraiser for Roger Stone the night before my hearing. At the time, he was fighting for his freedom after a malicious prosecution. It was true that I took a plea to a misdemeanor charge to avoid a fight with the federal government. That was a war that I knew I wasn't properly armed for—I had no experience defending myself in that arena. Attempting it seemed daunting, dangerous, and expensive.

I didn't dispute the crime because, at that moment, there was no point in fighting the system. There was also an ugly fight in probate court that I admit was accurate and undeniable.

To be honest, I was glad I went to prison. This is probably one of my crazier statements, but if I hadn't gone to jail, there wouldn't have been those sensationalized headlines. Without them, you wouldn't be reading this book—I chose to see an opportunity in this experience, while others predicted my failure.

I think that's part of the natural karma that has unfolded. The shots aimed in my direction weren't fatal; they only took me down temporarily, and I recovered stronger than before. The three-ring circus I experienced gave me a platform to tell my story. When it was happening, I reminded myself that the comeback could become greater than the setback. I just needed a little more patience.

It was strange to be publicly shamed and labeled a criminal. It was also strange to become a target of the cancel culture that I despised. I've had a few titles over my lifetime—daughter, mom, wife, CEO, and even Mrs. Florida—but being called a criminal was not something I'd ever considered, even in the months and weeks leading up to my incarceration.

This ordeal gave me more faith than I had previously. I knew there had to be a point where the road would be a dead-end for the people who attempted to silence me.

"Mrs. Florida looked relaxed and unperturbed, pleading guilty in U.S. district court." That statement was another speck of truth behind the headlines. I was unperturbed because life had taught me that the drama of an emotional moment is always temporary, and in the end, good always prevails over evil. This story isn't over yet, but the Florida sunshine has finally started to peek through the dark clouds of the last few years and the momentary hell has given way to fearlessness. The craziness of it all has allowed me opportunity to tell the story of what happened to my family and expose the truth hidden by fake news.

In reality, the nursing home was paid in full, despite the claim that I owed them money. The lawsuit that they waged against me was voluntarily dismissed a few months after I went to jail. The media wasn't interested in reporting this dismissal, the same way it was uninterested in how my mother died in that same nursing home. It was selective reporting—if it wasn't unflattering or sensational, then the media ignored it.

There is a real racket in the con, the lies, and the profitable game that is guardianship. You may or may not know about this swindle, but people are waking up to the reality that elderly victims are used as pawns for litigious profiteers.

When my news hit, there was no public outcry. Since then, the issue has become more visible through the #freebritney movement, spurred by Britney Spears and her conservatorship saga. Then there's the Netflix smash hit *I Care A Lot,* in which a vape-smoking guardian takes hostage of elderly victims for profit.

Previous documentaries on the subject have received very little publicity or attention. Families have demanded action for their relatives over the years, but it's a topic that the media and public often ignore, perhaps because the pain is not something anyone wants to deal with. Maybe the corruption of this system goes so deep, these organizations are able to silence the press. All of these stories seem to be ruled by a similar motive—the almighty dollar.

In my case, the elderly victim was my mother. Ours was journey of giving up our rights, and I got a hard, fast lesson on what happens when you lose control.

Nevertheless, I knew there had to be a silver lining. That belief was what kept me going. It got me through the dark moments of my mom's death, the loss of my freedom, and the massive legal bills that could have broken us financially. I could've gotten swept up in the short-term pain, but that would have given the devil what he wanted. I don't make deals with the devil, and I wasn't willing to give in to that to save myself.

My stint in the clink was self-surrender; there was no knock on the door, no takedown, and no handcuffs in the back of a cop car. I simply showed at the prison, and they took me in and locked me up. It was a pre-planned event. The whole thing was very surreal, like waiting for a surgical procedure you don't want to have, but that you know will save your life.

Of course, there was a big part of me that just didn't want to deal with it. I kept going on with my life as if it wasn't happening. In the weeks before, I made an unconscious choice to live in the moment. There were the usual events, dinners, and work engagements I continued with to distract myself. I simply could not allow my thoughts to be consumed with the chilling reality that the clock was ticking.

The papers created an alternate reality and reported that I was alone. Where were my husband, my kids? The reports painted a picture that I was abandoned or shunned by my family. The media was strategically laying the groundwork for my cancellation.

Missing from those headlines was my decision to take the hit alone and control what little I could. I wanted to shield my family from the media circus. I was a lone wolf in the courtroom and when I entered prison. The paparazzi snapped cover shots as I climbed the stairs with my lawyers by my side. That fateful climb sealed my fate as an inmate.

The term "self-surrender" makes the whole ordeal sound voluntary, but it was far from that. It felt more like an inescapable outside force placing pressure on me until I broke. I had no choice but to give in—there really wasn't another rational option.

Fighting against the government would have financially broken me and ripped my family apart. I needed the stress to end—I needed to stop the crazy train. According to my lawyers, it would take hundreds of thousands of dollars to fight with a not-guilty plea. That just wasn't in the cards. It was enough already. I never thought of it as giving up—simply put, I was giving in.

The prosecutor had created a three-ring circus in the courtroom—it was surprising that there wasn't a popcorn machine in the corner for spectators. The cast of clowns in included the nursing home director, a few cronies, and Democrat lawyers on the other side of my civil lawsuits. The magistrate well received the prosecutor as she conducted a courtroom ringmaster's act shuffling around in her bright purple pantsuit.

Several days before the circus, the premonitions started. I felt it in my gut that the ringmaster was going rogue. I knew somehow that she was going to throw her promises out. My attorney's reassurances were not comforting; the panic was setting in.

After it was over, it was all in the transcript—it was clear as day for anyone to review. The motion to stay was denied, and there was no chance to avoid the stay behind bars. The appeal my lawyers filed was just red tape moving slowly through the necessary ranks. The letters to the then Department of Justice Attorney General Bill Barr and the White House probably wouldn't yield any action before surrender.

The duration of the sentence appeared strategic; it was perhaps chosen for effect and optics. As I was a conservative commentator, there would be no Club Fed. Despite the lack of any priors, I received a thirty-day prison sentence for misappropriation of social security funds, a misdemeanor.

The jail was a towering, high-rise lockdown, with no fresh air and no sunlight. There would be no transfer to a Martha

Stewart-type minimum-security camp. My short sentence meant that they would hold me at a Federal Detention center in one of Miami's most dangerous neighborhoods.

FDC Miami is a maximum-security facility and a real concrete jungle in the city. I would be housed in the general population with murderers, gang members, and drug dealers. These would be my roommates. Before my surrender, I was advised that my public persona and political leanings would make it even more dangerous for me in this prison. I was at risk for my safety because of my positions—equal justice was not on the table for a Trump supporter in 2020.

That morning, it seemed the clock was on fast-forward. Before I was mentally prepared, it was already 9:00 a.m. I had about thirty minutes left until my freedom was stolen. As a high-profile celebrity attorney, my lawyer, Guy Fronstin, was more than familiar with the headlines and paparazzi. He rolled up to the valet at my building at 9:30 a.m. He was the only person who knew the ropes.

The night before the criminal hearing, I held a fundraiser for Roger Stone. At a private dinner after the fundraiser, I confided with him about my sentence. His advice was always great, and that night was no different. He looked at me and said, "You'll get back up from this stronger. They hate us because we make a difference."

I found comfort in his statement as we drove south on I-95 towards the jail. Guy's cell phone rings onto the Bluetooth, shattering an awkward silence as he speaks to a reporter. I can tell he feels guilty about his promises and reassurances. I know he tried, but he couldn't have calculated all the factors. I don't blame him. Despite the way things went down, he had the best intentions, but the culture and political climate had hit a new low, where the old strategies and best-laid plans didn't matter.

We rolled into the parking garage on the southside of the expansive judicial complex an hour before my scheduled surrender. I spent those last moments updating my profile picture on social media to a photo of me in a black and white striped prison costume. In the years before, charity events were a big part of my life, and the photo from the American Cancer Society Jail and Bail event seemed very fitting. (I had to make light of this somehow. Posting that comedic picture was slightly satisfying.)

There was a lot of waiting around—I sat on a small wooden bench as guards laughed with each other. My invisibility was evident as I overheard them discuss what they did the night before and had planned for the weekend. There was a break in their conversation to take fingerprints, then I heard a somewhat snarky comment on my newly manicured pink and white nails by a female officer. I wanted to respond with my signature brand of sarcasm but bit my tongue.

They snapped my mugshot in front of a height chart on the wall. This was a prison step and repeat, without the red carpet. I thought of this and smiled at the camera. A male officer acknowledged me for a half-second and remarked on my outstanding attitude.

After lunch and what seemed to be a shift change, a female officer appeared to lead me through another massive metal door to an expansive room where brown and green garments lined the shelves. The plastic bins below contained dollar store shower shoes. These shoes and brown knee-high socks were my footwear for the duration of my stay.

The wall to my right was lined with curtains separating small dressing rooms. These dressing areas gave a strange illusion of privacy. The guard behind me watched as I undressed; it was a raunchy strip show of sorts as I picked up each boob and turned to face her. She instructed me to turn around and spread my cheeks, then told me to squat and cough.

On the first round, I don't dip low enough. Exasperated, she said, "Again." The cavity expulsion exercise yielded no result. I was more annoyed than humiliated, and I asked the guard about a tip.

She gave a slight smirk as she handed me the stack of green and brown garments. The green jumpsuit was enormous. It's frayed edges on the bottom indicated the simple difference between women and men—women are missing the bottom part.

"What shoe size are you?" she asked, as she rummaged through a bin on the floor. There was the hollow sound of plastic slapping the concrete, and I noticed one of the pinkish-brown plastic sandals was significantly lighter than the other. (Strangely, they reminded me of a pair of Jimmy Choos that I once bought on sale. They had been on display for a long time, and the right shoe had been lightened by the sun in the store's window.) I slid the dollar store shoes over my socks.

I was then told to hop up onto an odd-looking body scanner, set up just in case the squat and cough allowed something to remain in a cavity. After placing your chin on a platform, the scanner scanned your head as you tilted it from side to side. My new attire-distributing friend brought in another guard when the machine didn't appear to work. After several minutes of troubleshooting, they collectively gave up. It crossed my mind that I could have brought in a shank or a small bottle of tequila.

I followed her out the door toward a set of jail cells. These looked exactly like what you would imagine—everything was an industrial shade of a minty green, if not a filthy beige or gray.

The concrete cell contained a metal toilet with an attached sink and single faucet. Around the walls were small wood benches.

The metal click locked the bars behind me. I heard the keys jingling on the chain from the guard's waist. I looked around at the aluminum sink and toilet combo for some toilet paper and felt a deep sense of relief when I found it. There was only cold water tinged with rust. I used water to wet the toilet paper and wipe the bench and the half wall. There was a tangible satisfaction in cleaning the cell, and it took ten minutes off the clock.

I expected the dirt, but nothing prepared me for the temperature. I unsnapped the jumpsuit to my waist, folded my arms inside and kneeled on the bench. I managed to stick my head inside the jumpsuit and maintained a facedown fetal position with my forehead and knees pressed against the hardwood. It was one of those times that it paid off to be petite.

All I thought about was the anger that I had toward the ridiculous circumstances that put me here. I reassured myself that this was rock bottom—there was only one way to go from here.

The passage of time was impossible to gauge behind bars. I heard the metal click, and I started to get up. The guard said, "Not yet." A pretty, young black girl was ushered in. She was wearing nice name-brand glasses. Her tattoos resembled a child's art and seemed to contradict the designer frames.

She sucked in her teeth and complained about the last time she was here. She paced beside me as I curled into a fetal position on the bench. Four or five hours passed, and men were being ushered into cells around us. The guards brought us a portable hospital curtain to block their view. More time passed, and several women were ushered in and with them came brown trays containing unidentifiable slop and cartons of milk. I was not yet desperate enough to eat and offered my milk to one of the larger occupants in the cell.

After the meal and more attempts to keep warm, there was an intake medical exam. A friendly, smiling doctor and a space heater were the first comforts that day. After she shut the door, I made as much conversation as I could just to stay in the confines of her space.

As we talked, she seemed confused. She said, "So they put you in a maximum-security detention center for a misdemeanor? Are you sure this isn't one of those 'insider' documentary things?"

Sadly, it wasn't.

Hours went by. It was late evening—the way we knew this was by seeing another shift of guards rolling in, which meant eight hours had passed. The jingling that I had become all too familiar with approached. A guard told us to line up and handed each of us a stiff, rolled blanket.

The men started to catcall as we were escorted from the curtained cell. The guards quickly ushered us through another massive metal door and into an elevator. We were told to face the back of it as we ascended upward. Its destination was a mystery, just like the passage of time. It was impossible to tell how high we climbed.

The doors opened behind us to the only women's unit. It sounded like a zoo from the hallway. There was an undisguisable clamor somewhere between screaming and laughter. Just inside the door, there were banks of retro payphones and cafeteria tables. It was just as cold as it was downstairs and smelled like disinfectant with an undertone of mold. As we walked in, a certain energy hit me. It was the feeling of being on a busy city street in a questionable area—you're scared stiff but stuck and have to deal with whatever you find around you.

We were lined up as another inmate in a green jumper greeted us. She was a tough-looking, short-statured woman with long braids and a shiny, gold smile. In her custodial position, she manned the supply closet by the entry door and handed each of us a roll of toilet paper, a toothbrush and toothpaste set, and a bar of soap. All the girls begin asking for pantyliners, which seemed strange at the time but made sense pretty quickly. (They were professionals, and I was the newbie.)

I looked around and realized that I was standing in the middle of a raised platform. It was almost like a stage in the center of two floors of cells. There were women on the lower floor peering through the railings to see who just came in. There was the sound of arguing in the distance and a clamoring of voices in Spanish and English. All of them ran together in the echo of the space.

A male guard yelled at us and directed the natives circling the platform to go back to their cells; he then ordered me to follow him. All eyes were on me as I exited the stage to the right, climbing a stairway to the second floor. Things became utterly chaotic when a group of Cuban women started to argue with the guard about where he was placing me and directed him to take me back down the stairs.

He reluctantly submitted to what they told him to do. I was too cold to wonder about the dynamic and his seeming lack of control. I was just anxious to get situated. We wandered back down to explore what rooms had open bunks.

A tall, thin white woman opened her door. "She can come in here," she said. He looked relieved to finish this task. He pointed in her direction and slammed the door behind me.

The woman was missing her front teeth apologized to me for her appearance, explaining that they were knocked out when she was arrested. Her name was Lynn. She was rail thin—I was chilled to the bone, and I couldn't imagine how cold she must be. She crouched down to the brick-colored footlocker on the broken linoleum floor and began her mission to help me. She proudly handed me a thermal undershirt. It was yellowed and shredded at the elbows, and the cuffs were ringed with dirt. I didn't care—I was just happy for her hospitality.

"You can take the top bunk," she said, crawling under the covers on her bed, fully clothed. I climbed up onto a thin foam mattress with no pillow. I unrolled the blanket, which revealed two flat sheets, one small hand towel, and a single brown wash-cloth. As I shivered, I made the bed; I pulled the sheet tight and tucked its edges. I looked around the room at the dirty walls and linoleum floor, and the single, leaking sink on the cluttered concrete counter. The two square vents above the toilet were rusted with black edges. I realized the black was a sprinkling of mold, and these vents were forcing the refrigerated air into the small cell.

My new roommate saw me shake as I wrapped the blanket around myself. "Don't worry. We cover the air vents with panty liners after they count us for the night. I've been in a few places like this one. I have a problem with drugs. I've been in and out of jail." Her straightforwardness was something I wasn't expecting.

As we waited for the final count that night, she told me her story. It was reminiscent of many stories that I heard that month. These were stories of people who had hard choices to make, and people who had made mistakes. In some cases, they were born into the system and spent large portions of their lives behind bars. They were people who lost control of their lives and lost their freedom. These women were mothers and grandmothers.

Their stories defined how they got to where they were on a journey that led me to stand before them. They were people just like you and me.

> *"It is said that no one truly knows a nation until one has been inside its jails. A nation should not be judged by how it treats its highest citizens, but its lowest ones."*
> —*Nelson Mandela*

Chapter 2 ───────────

Standing in a Swamp

In South Florida, anything greater than five miles west of I-95 is alligator country. It is swampland that has been filled over, far beyond the 'burbs. The landscape is dotted with retention ponds and canals, and the fill serves to keep the water table from rising. It's a coordinated effort to keep the swamp and its contents from surfacing. Florida developers have mastered the skill of making things look manicured, even when building on top of a swamp.

The proverbial swamp in D.C. co-mingles with real swampland in Florida. Politicians and political corruption run together into the Everglades. In my mind, it's a well-established process to keep the bodies buried.

What should be a peaceful goodbye to my mom was simply a facade hiding a darker truth. As I stood on the edge of the swamp, I looked over my shoulder and noticed the darkness was setting in, with help from the perpetual cloud cover that was set in motion during the events of the last few years.

I held onto my dad's ashes until she passed. I had imagined that I would take them to Saint Thomas, where they once spent their honeymoon. But now was not the time I could do that. The beauty of my mom's memory had quietly been stolen, just like her memories were stolen by Alzheimer's.

When my mom's dementia advanced, she had a fear of "robbers." She called me almost every day in a panic, spinning stories of potential threats. She was afraid of what they would do to her. She was prophetic, and we were naïve. She knew before we did. As her dementia progressed even further, she worried about lawyers and court cases that didn't exist. I would reassure her that these were just dreams. Flash forward to the present, and her demented dreams were all too accurate.

My thoughts ran fast through my mind and through the clouds. *Saint Thomas should have happened. I shouldn't be here. This is not how it was supposed to end.* I flashed back to memories of my parents' honeymoon pictures. Framed with a white border and scalloped edges, they were idyllic black and white snapshots taken on a steep cliff overlooking a lagoon at the beginning of their beautiful life together. They were married forty-seven years.

My parents always made things work—there was never another option. My mom's dementia started slowly; she became forgetful. There were plastic bags with random items strewn about their apartment. Sometimes, my dad's car keys went missing and found their way into one of those bags. My father's frustration was visible, but also fleeting. He would mutter and curse under his breath but still call her "dear" as he recovered a missing item.

I now stood at the VA cemetery next to the niches at a government-run quickie service. I'd been here before and knew the drill—it was a funeral assembly line. Beneath the cloud cover, I realized that, as the niche closed, a gate was opening. It wasn't a pearly gate to heaven for my mom, it was a gateway to purgatory for me against a gang of strangers who sought destroy the honor of her memory and discredit my validity as her daughter.

There was a weird stillness in the air; it felt heavy. I am usually never at a loss for words, but I was intensely quiet as we waited. So much was happening under the cloud cover of this particular Monday.

I was somewhat paralyzed as we waited in the numbered spaces. I talked to myself in my head, telling myself things that soothe me—*the weather is good, and she would want us to be at peace.* Optimism has always been my thing, but it has faded over the past few years, just like my mother's memories faded from Alzheimer's. I've been slapped in the face by a reality that is, at times, unbearable.

As we sat in the dark cloud of silence and waited in line for the procession to begin, I looked at my husband. He doesn't try to say anything, likely because he had no idea what to say. It seemed like a strange way to begin a memorial—in a car, silently waiting for the funeral procession to begin. Only our screwed-up government could make this a more agonizing process than it already was.

More negative thoughts crept in, but I attempted focus on the positive. *Keep moving, keep going.* The silence was deafening. I started to play around on my iPhone. I looked for music I thought my mom would appreciate, like Bach or Beethoven. They weren't a good choice—too classical and too sad. I settled for my mom's brand of popular music.

My husband looked at me and smirked. He knows most of my stories and how simple yet complicated my childhood was as the misfit daughter of cultured older parents who escaped the Holocaust.

I settled on Arlo Guthrie. He was my mom's favorite folk singer. Growing up, Arlo was a badass in a world of classical records and opera in our home. He was a folk singer, a hippie, and social justice fighter. (My mom had a hippie moment back in those days, as a social justice, freedom-fighting liberal.)

In 2019, social justice was slapped from the hands of conservatives like me. The conservative voice became the voice to shut down. Cancel culture had arrived. Any voice could be silenced by another's unwillingness to hear anything other than conformity to their thoughts and beliefs. I believe the fight against cancel culture and the war on free speech are the civil rights movements of our generation.

I had read a lot about Arlo, and I find his political leanings interesting. (I've read a lot in general; I am a purveyor of random facts and information. Luckily, most of it I can apply to my life.) Mr. Guthrie falls in line with many Americans, particularly baby boomers. He was always known for a left-leaning approach to American politics. In his younger years, during concerts, it was customary to hear him rant about his anti-Nixon, pro-drug stance. In 1984, he was the featured celebrity in George McGovern's campaign for the Democratic presidential nomination.

Going into the Bush years, he took a turn and became a registered Republican in 2008. He endorsed Congressman Ron Paul for the Republican Party nomination that year. He said, "I love this guy…Dr. Paul is the only candidate I know of who would have signed the Constitution of the United States had he been there. I'm with him because he seems to be the only candidate who believes it has as much relevance today as it did a couple of hundred years ago." He then told *The New York Times Magazine* that he was a Republican because he thought, "We had enough good Democrats. We needed a few more good Republicans. We needed a loyal opposition."

His thoughts are relatable. Although he didn't endorse Donald Trump, he did praise him for not relying on campaign donations. Again, a relatable sentiment. He may not be a Trump supporter, but he gets it. Arlo also made a statement about urging his fellow Americans to stop the current trend of guilt by association and look beyond the party names and affiliations. It's perplexing how we can't find a way to do that.

Civil rights, peace, and love are not representative of today's liberalism—the movement of the '60s was much more conservative. As I said earlier, my mom had a hippie moment. She fought for women's rights with the National Organization for Women (NOW) and marched on Washington D.C., all while wearing cool patterned slacks. (She got to appreciate that amazing 1960s fashion firsthand!) She was a liberal freedom fighter who had a wild side and hung out with artists on Fire Island.

As Arlo Guthrie's "City of New Orleans" played, we finally proceeded to drive in a neat little line through the cemetery. Here I was, at a funeral listening to a song related to a place where funerals are celebrated. Perhaps it was a sign that my mom wants her memory to be celebrated, too.

"City of New Orleans" has always been one of my favorites because Arlo was the only album beyond classical music in our home. He was my first storyteller. New Orleans seemed like a far-off, foreign place, and its magical energy and vibrancy were in stark contrast to the cemetery.

I come out of this comforting moment as we followed the leader in the golf cart. We were trailing behind in our respective cars through the expanse of the well-manicured, organized cemetery, with rows upon rows of deceased men and women. These were people whose lives were reduced to small marble plates on numbered divisions. I've seen too many of these places and experienced too much loss in the last few years. Now that loss includes both my parents.

It's pretty clear why my father's ashes remained in my shoe rack for as long as they did. It was almost more dignified to have him beside a pair of Louboutin stilettos, where I could see him every day, than behind an expansive stark marble wall. *He wouldn't like this,* I thought.

My dad was dedicated to our government but would be so disappointed with where we are today. In the moment, I was annoyed by the callous nature displayed by the workers at the cemetery but even more annoyed at the injustices in our government that I knew were brewing behind the scenes with me.

Where is justice? What's happened to the positive outlook? Not just for me, but in America. My parents were a product of the American dream, and I was lucky enough to be included in that story. From my father's service during the Korean War to his work with the Department of Defense in the 1950s, he was a true lover of American freedom.

At eleven, my dad didn't speak a word of English, but he landed at Cornell at the age of fifteen on a full scholarship. My mom, an immigrant girl from Brooklyn, was tranquil and street smart; she was a graduate of Brooklyn College who taught for a short time but chose to be homemaker. She was a throwback to a different time, and despite her days of marching for NOW and volunteering to teach immigrants English well into her later years, she dedicated herself to her husband and family. As much as my mom pretended to be progressive, she was more traditional than she would ever care to admit.

My parents were Democrats, but the Democratic Party wasn't what it is today. As my father aged, he became angrier at the changes he saw in liberalism and was always annoyed by the "lefties" that made the party look bad. My parents were Democrats, but they were still conservatives and would have been horrified at the current discussions of socialism. As children, they both escaped the Nazi occupation of Austria with their families. When I first brought my parents to Florida, they were still doing well. We would spend evenings on their couch watching their favorite show on Fox News, *The O'Reilly Factor*. My mom would sometimes pretend to be annoyed, all the while mentioning how good-looking and smart she thought Bill was. My dad would refer back to his childhood in Austria and how America was going down the toilet with these new radicals.

He saw it coming; he knew where we would be. I didn't see it back then. I admit, I was slow to get it, but now I'm waking up to reality.

I stood next to the expansive wall of lives, reduced to cold marble plaques adorned with crosses and the Star of David. They were American heroes, many of them from the Greatest Generation like my parents. I scanned all the names that I don't know, including surnames as nondescript as Smith and as familiar as Leibowitz. I'm zoned out, probably because I wanted to shift the emotion welling up inside me. Sadness makes me uncomfortable—it makes my husband uncomfortable too. My oldest daughter, however, is opposite us on the emotional scale and is in full breakdown mode. As I quietly stood there, I felt like she was judging because of my lack of emotion. She and my mom had a special bond. She got my mom, and my mom got her. It's definitely a grandma thing. It's much easier to be relatable one generation removed.

Here in this overly organized place with these neat little niches, I kept thinking that I didn't organize this well. Their lives should be more than just a marble slab of people's names. The service should be more reflective of the importance of their lives, especially as I knew there were characters intent on bringing me down who have no regard for my mother's life or my family's well-being.

I was distracted. I knew it and felt it. I glanced over at the government workers. They look annoyed. We were taking way too long to say goodbye. After all, the memorial was a government process. That some people wanted big government was hard to follow. I kept thinking of the callousness of it all, of becoming just another numbered person and just how much has changed in the past few years.

I tried not to let the dark thoughts resurface and resigned myself that it was time to let go and let my parents be together. I closed my eyes to try to bring in some peace and reminded myself that everything happens for a reason. My husband began to read the Kaddish, in Hebrew, as the niche was being closed by the workers anxious to move on to the next gig. I felt like my dad was in my ear saying, "Can you believe this bullshit?"

"The measure of a decent human being is how he or she treats the defenseless."
—Bill O'Reilly

Chapter 3 ———————

Gargoyles and Guardians

*I*n the days after my mom's death, negative thoughts crept in over and over. *How could anyone let this happen? Did my decisions lead to this outcome? How will I ever move forward from this? How could I be so naïve?* The stress was always present, and I was filled with a silent rage that had no outlet. Opening social media first thing in the morning was probably the wrong way to start my day.

A conservative news reporter mumbled on the bedroom flat screen as my husband banged around in the closet. He was always searching for socks or T-shirts that have been in the same place for years. As he handed me my coffee, I forgot to thank him, which he was quick to point out. *Yes, I'm the asshole.*

Seven years together is not comparable to my parents' legacy, but it's a step further than my last two marriages. This one will beat the duration of second marriage in a year, which was far longer than the first.

My husband routinely points out that my days often start on the wrong foot. He's expressed how looking at social media and the news as soon as we wake up is a bad idea and how I am not the same person that I used to be. He's 100 percent right. I'm not—not even close.

As he readied himself for work, I was engaged in a politics and social media war on my phone. Strangely, it was a pleasant distraction. I sometimes wondered if he comprehended what else is going on. The storm was brewing swiftly behind the scenes; social media and news were like a vacation from reality. The real world caused me to bite my tongue so hard that I could taste blood.

Images flashed in my head—the wounds, the blood, the flesh eaten away. The things I witnessed are things you just can't block out. Every memory shook me to my core. I could be distracted online. Commenting feverishly on something took those horrific visuals out of my mind, at least momentarily. (Soapboxing can be therapeutic; as much as I sometimes judge keyboard warriors, I get it. It's an outlet. Exhibiting passion online just helps to suppress real feelings.)

When I came up for air, I realized my husband left without saying goodbye. I wasn't necessarily upset that I missed it. I just didn't want to be blamed for screwing something up and went back to the task at hand.

Someone was trolling on my public page. *Are you serious? Why are you defending this congresswoman? How can you not see with your own two eyes what is happening to in our own backyard?*

Like so many other American cities, West Palm Beach is deteriorating at the hands of Democrat Party leadership and is at risk of becoming a shithole if we aren't careful. Parking my car at the downtown television studio has become risky over the past few years. Most of the homeless are only panhandling, but others are visibly mentally ill or under the influence, to the point of being dangerous. Nightfall brings a fear reminiscent of New York City in the early 1980s.

The congresswoman in question is responsible for establishing downtown West Palm Beach as a sanctuary city, which resulted in the loss of law and order. She is just another career politician—a white-suited feminist wannabe, promoting an agenda that defies our American ideals, all the while driving around in a luxurious black car with an entourage. This deranged mafia of idiots who continue to vote her in and the financial support backing her are in our backyard. They are, at best, misled and misdirected, or worse, they are blind and incredibly stupid.

I found myself infuriated at the whole Facebook thread. It was hard to tell if it was a real person or a troll. I told myself that it must be a troll, as no actual human could be this stupid.

Unfortunately, I knew better; these people are real. The corruption and deep state are real, and the swamp is everywhere. It's not just in Washington D.C. or even in the Everglades, out by the alligators. It's deep, murky, smelly, and ugly, and we're surrounded by it.

After losing my mom under horrific circumstances and at the hands of the ultimate corruption, I couldn't keep my eyes off my phone. I wasn't waiting for the next Facebook thread or social media notification—I was anticipating the call that I wish wasn't necessary but couldn't be more important.

I told myself that I wouldn't fuck this part up. We got to her before they took her. I did finally get her out, but it was too late to save her life. They hog-tied me.

The images are still fresh and constantly play out like a graphic horror movie; I still see her eaten flesh and rigid body.

It was like rigor mortis had set in, but she was still alive. I tried desperately to get help, but no one would listen. Maybe the court-appointed guardian blocked my number. It was the only explanation for the lack of connection. The calls that wouldn't even go through. *How did I allow them to appoint her?* I couldn't help but blame myself.

To think the word "guardian" could mean anything less than a guardian angel was one of the biggest shockers in my life. Perhaps my childhood perception of the world had skewed my ability to see reality. In the crime-ridden New York City of my youth, the Guardian Angels were freedom fighters. They rode the subway wearing their signature red berets and white T-shirts. I was in awe of them and their ability to unite and fight.

As a little girl, I often perched myself on our striped, brown coach and stared into the black and white 19-inch television. My dad would read the paper, putting it down for a moment or two to comment on Mayor Koch and the street-smart crime fighters. The green shag rug beneath us was a dumping ground for the discarded newspapers that had been read. Older newspapers were piled several feet high in the corners of the room, like Grecian columns or pedestals that I had seen in old movies. I imagined our little gray Tudor on a cedar-lined street in Teaneck, New Jersey to be my newspaper palace. Its decorative columns were made of newspapers, and the detailed glass doorknobs on the stained wooden doors were diamonds.

The Guardian Angels were the superheroes of my childhood in Bergen County, New Jersey. The New York City subway was the most dangerous mass transit system in the world in the late 1970s. The Guardian Angels were real-life vigilantes; they were the living "boom-pow" of a *Batman* cartoon. These angels in berets wore shirts with a logo of an all-seeing eye inside a pyramid on a winged shield. I remember thinking that it was just like the Masonic symbol from my dad's lodge. It was a secret society, after all—maybe the Guardians were Masons. Maybe my dad was one of them. He seemed to have a lot of secrets, despite being a man who loved to talk.

Watching the Guardian Angels in action was beautiful. They'd burst into action to stop an armed robbery or beat the pulp out of a bad guy and make a citizen's arrest. Vigilante justice took over when it was obvious the system was failing. This was the way things were supposed to be. It was simple, impactful, and understandable. The bad guys don't win—truth and justice do prevail. The world made sense. I knew the subways, and I knew this world.

We went into New York City pretty often. After my fourth birthday, my mother never drove again. A fender bender in her blue Dodge Dart coming off Route 4 was the excuse. The accident had terrified her. It was her fault; she was an admittedly bad driver, and there was nothing more to discuss.

After that incident, I had a mother who didn't drive. There would be no more sitting backward in a station wagon as she picked up my friends to go to gymnastics with me. We were mass transit bound from that point on. (She was a city girl anyway.) There were now schedules to read and decipher; we had to organize ourselves to get where we wanted to go.

New York was chaotic and very different from my treelined street. It was dirty and scary, but magical. I felt empowered by the slight feeling of fear. My Brooklyn-raised mom became transformed as we crossed the majestic George Washington Bridge at the 178th Street bus terminal into Washington Heights, the neighborhood my father had grown up in. It had since become a dilapidated neighborhood in "Fear City," as the New York Police

Department had coined it in 1980, a time in which there was a warning to tourists not to go out after sunset.

But we weren't mere tourists. After a fifteen-minute bus ride, we were natives. In those days, my Thom McAn shoes were well-worn from pounding the pavement. As we walked through the tunnels, we would see homeless junkies lying beside the trenches, which became public urinals that led under the streets of Manhattan.

I was always instructed to move quickly and not make eye-contact with anyone. My mother had a plan for when a mugger approached us. (Remember, she was a real-life city girl.) If she perceived someone as a threat, she would act like a crazy person and begin talking to herself. I wouldn't even see them coming, but she did. I knew danger was approaching when I heard her begin rambling. She would mumble in nonsensical patterns. Maybe this was prophetic—she rambled nonsensically when dementia took over in her later years.

We briskly moved through the tunnels and down the stairway. This was the prequel to the main event of standing on the platform for the downtown A-train. My mother would remind me that people get pushed. She'd say, "Don't lean over and look for the train. Some robbers will push you onto the tracks. Even if you see me do it, never do it. I'm from Brooklyn, I know what I am doing."

Every time she leaned over to look, I would cringe, anticipating her impending doom. I was always relieved as the graffiti-adorned train would pull in. We had, once again, escaped a horrific, painful, slow death. As the squealing, silver monster opened its doors, people pushed and shoved with total disregard for everyone's safety, including their own. I'd watch elderly people and wonder how they could make it on and off the train—there was always danger lurking right next to them.

My mom's instructions were like a song that you can't get out of your head: "Just move quickly. Don't make eye contact. Act crazy." If things got really bad, I was to wail out a high-pitched scream. This seemed rational and very doable.

Normally, my mother's indistinguishable mumbling was enough to keep the bad guys at a distance—they were afraid of the demented. This wasn't the case later in life; legal predators were fearless and saw an opening in my mother's weakness. However, when I was a child, my mom's diversion plan was consistent and seemed to work.

Sometimes when things weren't kosher in our subway car, we'd move between them to another. It was dangerous while speeding through dark, dingy tunnels under the city. I made it into a game by inserting myself in a "movie" of my life. How many cars would we move through until I could spot them? I wasn't thinking of the robbers or bad guys. I was thinking of the smart street warriors who wore red berets with the all-seeing eye on their shirts.

The Guardian Angels had no hesitation in taking a man down. Their training in martial arts was a quiet power. They also trained in first aid, CPR, law, conflict resolution, and communication. There was no lack of diversity in these descended Angels; there was a commonality of good people of every age and race.

My father said that Mayor Koch was a mensch for his position on the group he initially opposed. As citizen involvement and outreach increased, he reversed his stance; he was a politician who listened to what his constituents wanted. The voices of the people who wanted law and order became too loud to ignore.

As we moved through the train cars, I would seek the Angels out. They were my up close and personal American heroes. Their bright red berets were a signal of what was good in America—the black and white television in my house didn't come close to matching the vibrant color in New York City. Its bustling, beautiful energy was never far away from my little suburban home.

In my present life, the phone rang. I didn't have this number saved, but I knew who it was. It was the call I've been anticipating and dreading. I tell myself it will bring closure and believe there will be justice in the end. I took a deep breath and answered.

"It's worse than you explained," the doctor that had performed the autopsy said. "I'm sorry about your mom. Do you have a lawyer? From a medical standpoint, it's definitive. The cause of death wasn't Alzheimer's, as stated on the death certificate by the medical examiner. I'm so sorry. It will be in my report."

I asked her several questions as my head spun. "Were the sores that bad? How much pain was she in? She had pneumonia. There were bruises on her face!"

I paced in my bedroom, angry. *How could this happen with a guardian standing by? How could this be? Where were the nurses, the caregivers, and the staff?*

I had almost convinced myself that I had imagined what I saw weeks earlier. My husband and I stood in horror at my mother's bedside with a calm and collected hospice nurse. A covert phone call had resulted in us being ushered into the facility. The hospice nurse rolled my mother on her side and pulled back the covers and what we saw will forever be burned into my mind. Her flesh eaten away with bones exposed. There were holes stuffed with gauze, oozing fluid.

"The facts will be in the report" the doctor said. "I brought my mother with me to perform the autopsy; she assists me sometimes. It took several hours. There was a lot to cover."

As she talks the guilt overwhelmed me, and I started questioning everything I did. I replayed the last several months and the times we desperately tried to get help over and over again. *How did this happen? How did I allow them to steal my freedom and my mother's soul?* The evil that had lurked for so long was now making me question my sanity. She didn't deserve this.

I looked down at my Thom McAn shoes once we were off the subway walking through the city. There was so much to take in both on the streets. I often looked up at the buildings—their rooftops always seemed to have more personality than what was at eye-level. My paternal grandmother lived in one of those buildings on the Upper West Side. It was adorned with gargoyles to keep evil spirits away.

My grandparents' apartment was far from kid friendly. My grandmother was a strong-willed, tough lady who only spoke German, a language that I was never able to grasp. Their apartment was a little too far from Central Park, so my playground when we visited was Grant's Tomb. It was a living testament of gratitude for the man who ended the bloodiest conflict in American history. Grant was the president who healed the nation after the Civil War and made rights for all citizens a reality. My father would delight in telling me about this time in American history in very vivid detail, and a visit to this concrete playground completed the picture.

President Grant had destroyed the Ku Klux Klan (KKK) and signed several acts to protect the rights of minorities. My father compared this to taking down the Nazis. WWII and its subsequent evils had been the reason for his immigration to America, the land of freedom, truth, justice, and liberty. He would remind me just how lucky I was to be born here. He would tell me there was justice in America and how President Grant was responsible for establishing the United States Department of Justice. I was enamored with Grant; he was one of the good guys, justice was fair, and America was free.

Across from Grant's Tomb was The Riverside Church, a neo-Gothic masterpiece adorned with a motherlode of gargoyles. As we walked through the colossal wood doors beneath the carved saints to light a candle in memory of those lost, my father reminded me of how good Christians had saved so many Jews in his childhood home of Austria.

Back on my phone call, the doctor didn't know what else to say. Her words were reduced to medical terminology that I couldn't absorb with my emotions tanking. I hang up. I was frozen and not sure if I was paralyzed by grief, fear, or a combination of both. Perhaps it was just a reaction to what I knew was around the corner.

"Keep moving. Move quickly," I heard my mother say. I knew for sure it was her spirit tugging at me. *How will I get through this? What's next? Could it possibly get worse?* If only I had placed some gargoyles above her bed at the nursing home, maybe I could have kept the danger away.

I then realized my war has just begun.

> *"To maintain peace in the future, it is*
> *necessary to be prepared for war."*
> —*Ulysses S. Grant,* Personal Memoirs
> of U.S. Grant: All Volumes

Chapter 4

Trapped in a Box

"You can come to pick up the box," the voice said on the other end of the line.

The box? Really? I responded sarcastically with a great, big "thanks."

People's lives are reduced to boxes. Their memories are stacked on top of each other, like the boxes in the marble wall at the cemetery and the boxes in my storage unit. We become another box. Box it up, get it out, and seal up the memory.

Why would I even want to go back to that nursing home? It's a hell hole, I thought. *The fucking balls you have to call me to come to get her stuff after you heartlessly let her die. You're a bunch of goddamn monsters.*

The halls of that place were stark, old, and smelled of a mixture of urine and despair. They reminded me of the New York City subway tunnels of my youth. The facility was a hard place to venture into, even when there was someone you loved inside. It was a place that sucked away dignity.

The facility's uniformed staff was emotionless. The workers' hard surfaces matched their hardened hearts. They moved in slow motion with utter disregard for everyone.

I'm not going back there to retrieve a box of photos. No, thank you, I have enough boxes. I couldn't go back to the facility once she was gone. It was simply too painful.

In the last year, all I saw here were clouded eyes and lack of connection. She was unable to speak. She couldn't express anything at all. I would often question if her soul was still there. Maybe she was already at peace on the other side, and her brain just sputtering along, making electrical connections to keep her body alive. This was a comforting thought over the alternative of awareness without the ability to communicate.

These were once vibrant people with families, lives, careers. They were strangers out in the world, moving swiftly together to get where they needed to go. They had grabbed a seat on the bus of life. They were people bustling through their hectic days who were now confined to a bed or hunched over in a chair. If they were lucky, there was a picture frame or two next to their beds with images of people they don't know anymore. Some were like my mom, unable to speak. One woman put a stuffed animal on her lap, petting it repetitively. Another screamed and was left to cry. She was a baby, left alone with no one to listen.

My mom knew it would happen to her. She predicted it, and it played out like a pre-determined fate. The shadows were creeping in. She was always fearful after her childhood escape from the Nazi occupation; if malevolence didn't overtake her before, then it would come to steal her memories. She watched it with her own eyes before the clouds rolled in for her to her mother.

My parents were throwbacks—the clock had stopped for them somewhere along the line after they came to America to find freedom. Their lack of advancement into the present day was, at many times, a blessing. It was also a walk back into an easier time.

In my early childhood, there was no FM radio or color television. We didn't even have an eight-track player to play the latest Bee Gees or Donna Summer hit. We would venture to the library to listen to music headphones in the children's department. The latest technology hadn't entirely caught up inside our little, gray, two-bedroom Tudor house with the glass doorknobs.

However, from early morning to evening, there was a soundtrack to every summer in Teaneck. Cicadas emitted a comforting buzz from the tops of the cedars lining the street. Their song was just as much a part of our summer as fireflies, Yankees baseball, and our annual block party on Grace Terrace. As my mom's memories began to fade, she still had these. They were on a kind of an automatic replay, and they were also my memories.

In summer 1979, I would put my Thom McAn red sandals with white bottoms neatly away, each day. I wanted to preserve them for as long as I could, and red was my very favorite color. These were the sandals that had pounded the pavement on the many miles we had already walked.

It was a summer filled with regular trips to the city, but there was a bigger adventure that awaited us in Washington, D.C. Jimmy Carter was still president, and there was a buzz of excitement in my house over the 1980 election. The newspaper columns stood high with political headlines.

After school was out for the summer, I begged my parents for a clock radio. It was a luxury item that they didn't think I needed, as I had a wind-up alarm clock with two bells in perfect working order. I made a compelling testimony and convinced them that this was the key to being responsible and getting up earlier. A clock radio was simply essential. I had won the argument—we soon ventured to RadioShack for my "early birthday present."

It was a flip clock radio, with brown plastic casing had those numbers on little flaps, but it was more than that—I t represented my independence. It even had FM, which was a foreign concept to me. At that time, there was only AM radio in my world and only talk radio in my dad's dark gold Plymouth Valiant with the contrasting white vinyl top.

This was the only sound beyond our intellectual conversations about history or math as we drove out to Brooklyn to my maternal grandmother's house. We heard the hum of the background static against tiny voices as we trekked across the Throgs Neck Bridge on our regular holiday trips to Great Neck, Long Island. It was there we would visit my mom's sister and my cousins.

Before that summer, talk radio was the only radio that I knew. I was taught that news and information were vital to a good conversation. The traffic jams were long, the summers were hot, and the pollution permeated through the rolled down, cranked windows into the car. As you sat on the highway, you were unable to move faster than anyone around you.

In my little blue bedroom with the yellow patterned vinyl tile floor, Don Imus on WNBC 66 was my rebellion. In our living room, the radio station's commercials played on our black and white television. WNBC's rank as the number two station in New York City was something it embraced. There was power in that second ranking; and station executives used it as a marketing opportunity.

The commercial started with their headliner, Don Imus, and featured several sets of twins in matching outfits saying how much they loved the station. "Working My Way Back to You" the new Top 40 hit by The Spinners was the jingly background to the catchy commercial. Its voiceover said, "66 WNBC, the twin station is twice as much fun. Twice as many winners, twice as many prizes, twice as many chances to win. I love the music on WNBC because they play...." cut to The Spinners' song.

I was immediately hooked—the cute sets of twins were the cherry on top. The thought regularly crossed my mind that maybe I had a twin that I didn't know about yet. Perhaps, somewhere out in the world, there was someone who looked like me. I certainly didn't resemble any of my cousins or other family members, with their dark hair and predominantly Jewish features.

My favorite radio station opened up a world of music, something beyond my mother's introduction to "popular music" as she knew it from Arlo Guthrie. Don Imus of Imus in the Morning was the first ever "shock jock" and headliner for New York City's flagship station. "WNNNNBCCC" was the drawn-out, booming slogan. Imus's edgy sarcasm was a new brand of personality in my universe and was my first clue that there were possibilities for people with shitloads of character and a rebellious edge. Imus was clever, funny, and smart. I was inspired and enamored. Radio was magical; it was my little brand of rebellion.

One day, in mid-August, I switched on the radio and noticed his voice had changed. He was more stoic, sad, and not the "jerk" that my father would comment about. His voice was low and emptied of its usual energetic tone. It made me a little uncomfortable.

I soon discovered there was a tragedy that morning, and it felt like it was my tragedy, too. New York Yankee catcher Thurman Munson was dead. This hit close to home—I felt like he was the first person that I knew who died. I had watched him with my dad just days before at the game.

Munson, a private pilot, had taken off from the Akron-Canton Regional Airport. On his approach, he took too long to drop his landing gear and crashed just before the runway. This happened in broad daylight in full view of motorists driving on I-77 near Canton, Ohio. I could picture it like I was on the highway sitting in traffic in the back of our Plymouth Valiant. However, this happened far off in Ohio, a place I had never been. I still felt this was my tragedy.

This was real and impactful. Watching him on the field and television, I felt like I knew him. His recognizable mustache was just like my dad's. He was approachable and would talk to fans. He was the celebrity next door, just across the George Washington Bridge and a quick ride to the Bronx.

I was thrown and shaken. My mother tried to console me by telling me that I didn't know him. This made me feel even worse, like my not knowing him made my pain meaningless. She told me that it was okay to be sad but that I needed to be upset for his family; this was their loss.

I rummaged through my dresser drawers, searching for something black to wear. I settled on pair of dark green shorts and a brown terry cloth top. There was an apparent lack of black in my wardrobe, but I needed my outfit to convey a message of mourning for my friend and baseball great. This loss was my first death.

His funeral would be held at the Canton Memorial Civic Center in Canton, Ohio. Based on the location and my mother's overall callousness towards my mourning, I quickly realized there was no chance that we were attending the services.

The game that night at Yankee Stadium was broadcast on WPIX 11. Even in the rainy weather that had blanketed the city, Yankee Stadium was packed as the home team paid tribute to the great Thurman Munson. Stadium flags were at half-staff, and the Yankees exited their dugout with their hands on their hearts. Cardinal Terence Cooke began praying to give our brother, who was a good family man, peace in Heaven, forever and ever. The tribute ended with "America the Beautiful," and it was the first time that song had given me goosebumps. I understood that this was America coming together in mourning. His life had value and meaning—it didn't matter that I didn't personally know him. The crowd in the stadium stood and delivered a long standing ovation. Long live the great Thurman Munson!!

I was thinking of my mother at the end of her life. Why was she so disposable to them? She wasn't a stranger. They knew and saw her. It made me shudder when I thought about it: *Were there others? Were we the only family that they had disregarded? Was I still hog-tied like I was before her death?*

I felt that I was still tied up with invisible ropes. These were the same kind of ropes that had been used to stop me from fighting back, speaking up, and exposing them. I was smarter from this tragedy—I was finally waking up to the reality of how many things were connected. I realized the past year had been a series of connected mistakes and events.

My mother's death was their fault, as evidenced by the autopsy. It was a glaring testament to the lack of care in nursing homes. Clear neglect took her, not Alzheimer's disease. *If I hadn't made mistakes, could I have saved her? Would she still be here? Would her few remaining memories have still been intact, frozen in that place in my childhood that we shared?* My thoughts spin, and my fury rages. I hide behind the smiles for photos on the red carpets, the celebrity interviews, and behind the cameras in the television studio. I am telling myself that I must move quickly and keep moving.

After Munson's death, my dad drove us out to Brooklyn for the weekend. During the week, he was at work, with his black Samsonite briefcase and porkchop sideburns, wearing something polyester, with a wide patterned tie.

That humid day began on the bus with my mom. I had to wake her up that morning. She had a headache and had overslept. This wasn't unusual. I was okay—I was responsible for myself. I had my alarm clock to wake me up. I strapped on my red sandals and, with my stool handy, I made her a cup of tea on the gas stove. I was going to get us moving. I packed the striped tote bag, which held history books to read on the bus and tissues for multiple purposes. I put out umbrellas to shield us from the rain.

Acid rain was a big concern back then. I knew all about it through reading *The New York Times* with my dad each morning. My dad was a chemical engineer and understood the impact of these developments. The assistant administrator for research and development at the Environmental Protection Agency, Stephen J. Gage, told the National Commission on Air Quality that a "hazy glob" of pollutants covered much of the U.S. between summer showers. Commission head Senator Gary Hart (a Colorado Democrat) said, "Acid rain is a particularly alarming demonstration of the simple adage that what goes up must come down."

The Democrats were concerned about the environment, and it was a regular topic of conversation in our home. If acid rain could damage artificial objects, what was it doing to people? I had asked my father if it was the acid that had caused mom's headaches? Could the chemicals all build up inside her and cause this?

I got ready up in my little blue room, listening to the latest Top 40 hit from the Bee Gees on my trusty radio. I was always excited when a good song came on—back then, radio certainly wasn't on-demand. You'd put up with what other listeners wanted to hear until you heard your favorite music.

The night before, I pulled out the basket of bus schedules from the bookshelf in my wooden headboard, painted in trendy avocado green. It was essential to be as prepared as possible. I knew that we had to be at the bus stop down on Route 4 on-time. All the buses we rode were predictable. Some were always late, some were on time, some were early. We would leave the house in the morning at 9:16 sharp, as this bus was always on time. I allowed for extra time if we needed it.

On the way out, my mom would inevitably check the gas stove five times to make sure she hadn't left it on, then she'd check that she didn't leave the iron on or plugged in. She always made sure the backdoor was locked to keep out potential robbers. Our routine was repetitive and predictable.

I set the alarm, laid out my outfit, and packed my yellow cardigan sweater with the embroidery on the front and back and red, beaded plastic buttons that matched my sandals. It was lightweight and just fancy enough to help me feel put together.

My maternal grandmother had brought it back from her trip to Miami Beach the past winter. With her beautiful Austrian accent, she was well-traveled, stylish, and modern. She would spend the season at the Fontainebleau or the Eden Roc. The presentation of this embroidered sweater was meaningful; for once, I got a better gift than my year-older cousin. She always seemed to get something more significant than I did. It was always apparent that she had some sort of an edge on me when it came to our grandma. The sweater made me look pretty and stylish, and my grandmother was happy that it was my favorite.

I made sure my mom was up, and her tea was ready. I then made sure that we would get there on schedule. That morning, it took longer than usual to catch our breath, as we ran to the platform to catch the train. Once we were in, the doors on the train car slammed shut with their trademark creaking sound. It was packed with people—a real rolling sardine can. There was no option to keep moving through cars today. We were trapped; I couldn't move an inch. The heat was overwhelming, and the air was heavy.

The train bobbed, weaved and screeched through the tunnels with its lights flickering. There were no red berets with white shirts—no angel wings and an all-seeing eye. This weekday, it was simply too crowded with straphangers to see more than a few people in front of us. I impishly smiled at a long-haired, bell-bottom-wearing teenager sharing the pole with us as the train barreled along. I looked at her hand, and those of the others who grabbed the pole bare-handed. Between my hand and the pole was tissue from our tote bag—my mother was careful about this. There were germs and risks everywhere.

The trusty A train roared downtown. We'd jump onto the B soon, following the alphabetic sequence. It was a game of sorts— the letters were usually an indication of where the trains went. "A" was the first letter of the alphabet, and it was always the first train we got on from the bus station. The "B" train downtown was for Brooklyn and uptown for the Bronx. Some were more cryptic. We'd take the E to Astoria, Queens where my paternal aunt lived. I imagined that this stood for Elizabeth, as in Queen Elizabeth.

Getting around was a constant hustle with a parent who didn't drive. This was a process that none of my suburban friends seemed to relate to. The planning of a trip consisted of details, schedules, strategy, and execution. We didn't have much free will in this instance; we were always at the mercy of the schedule. I imagined that having a car was real freedom. When I was a teenager, like my friend's sisters, freedom would finally be attainable. Emerging from the darkness of the underground, we exited the tunnel into Brooklyn. As we approached the brightness, we were blinded until our eyes adjusted. I imagined that this was like the tunnel that people saw when they died. Maybe this was what my friend Thurman Munson saw when he died. Maybe it's what my mom saw as she withered away in that cold room almost forty years later. Maybe she felt peace in seeing the light, knowing that all darkness comes to an end, and heaven is a reality.

That day, as we headed to her old stomping grounds in Brooklyn, heaven was the intersection of Sheepshead Bay and Manhattan Beach.

"I can't move, I can't move."
—*The last words of Thurman Munson*

Chapter 5

The Storm Begins

It was raining a Florida kind of rain. When it rains in Florida, it's usually not for long—it's like a burst of emotion. There's a downpour, thunder, and lighting, then within an hour, the sun is usually back out. The darkness never lasts for long.

I had so much to do, and I was trying to balance it all. I felt like I was spinning plates on sticks, with one bound to fall and break. *Which will it be? What is going to drop first?* Just like that Florida thunderstorm, I frequently exploded with anger, fighting with my husband over things that don't make sense. I was in a heap of rage as he suited up and headed out for the day. He didn't even ask about the pocket square.

That morning, Instagram was my outlet. I posted a picture with my hands, flashing the gesture Nixon made famous as a tribute to my friend Roger Stone. I moved on to defend him from the morning's internet trolls. "Better to be infamous than never to be famous at all," his *Stone's Rules* quote quieted the anxiety swirling around in my brain and comforted me for the moment.

I was typing so feverishly that by the time I grabbed my coffee, it's ice cold.

I fucking hate what happened to him. It's such a tragedy. *Don't they understand he's a human being?* The headlines reduced him to some dark-cloaked political figure. Politics aside, he's a father, a grandfather, a friend, and someone I respect. Roger's public persona is so misunderstood. The person takes time to listen to strangers during dinners and book signings. He's a marketing genius of sorts and has a wealth of historical knowledge. He's someone I find very inspiring.

They've gagged him; they've taken away his ability to fight back against injustice. He has no social media—no nothing. How can this be happening in America?

The early morning raid where they dragged Roger from his home would have reminded my father of the Gestapo. I often think about his strength when I saw him on the courthouse steps later that day and remind myself that I should be strong, no matter what they throw at me. *#rogerstonedidnothingwrong. What the fuck?*

Maybe my husband was onto something—waking up to social media was probably not the best idea for me. I switched to the laptop to update my website with some videos of this week's international news. I smirked as I uploaded a segment of me on RT International. *Russia, Russia, Russia. When will they let it go already?* This collusion narrative the press continues to spin is insanely stupid. The media even shifted to Chinese collusion for a minute, dragging in Mar-a-Lago and potential espionage charges that didn't stick. What could be next?

I was getting phone notifications non-stop. *The Miami Herald* called, again. I decline the call. *It can wait*, I tell myself. *I don't feel like I have it together yet.* At least my website was updated, and my latest news commentary was uploaded. Things looked good on the screen—that was a plus. Behind the scenes, however, there's was a void. I was scared and struggling.

It's not just my mom who has left us—others have also gone. Who would I call in a moment like this? Who would listen to me explain why Roger was mistreated? Who would agree with my latest political rantings? Who would listen to my struggle over my mom's death and my looming problems? Who would end the call telling me to be nicer to my husband?

A person who cared about her and visited her when he didn't have to—a person, who had been there, who had been my husband. But in a moment, he was gone. He was a guy who would bail me out in the middle of the night, if I needed it. He was my crusader, my one phone call, and my big Italian tough guy.

He was gone in a second; the world lost a little light less than a year ago. Now another phone call of mine will go unanswered.

As I was losing my mom, I was picking up his pieces. Our bad relationship left the house in shambles. It was the house my kids grew up in—the first house that we bought together while we were engaged, during the real estate bubble. It was an overpriced mistake, a bad decision that was my fault. I got in my car and drove out west, out to the alligators, to cookie-cutter suburbia.

I found it therapeutic to clean up his mess somehow. It was almost like he was still there. There was no way to make sense of it all. He wasn't the same person that I married—that much was evident. It was all very confusing, and I blamed myself.

How could I have not seen the signs? His girlfriend, the one he would constantly claim was "on her way out," worked in a rehab. Now that he's gone, she seems to delight in playing the victim in the wake of his death. Her first words from the night he died are still ringing in my head. She said she hoped I didn't "blame her." Blame her! Why would I blame her? However, less than a year later, that blame started to fester.

As I cleaned, I zoned out. We had many happy memories in this house. I thought about the swimming pool he spent most weekends by with a Miller Lite in hand. I thought about his stupid, loud-mouthed singing and his overindulgences. That big a personality equaled big risk.

I needed to face reality; I needed to know what happened. I knew it was an overdose from the toxicology report, but it was just so hard to grasp. Not him—a fentanyl overdose seemed like something akin to what a heroin addict would experience, like the junkies laying in the graffiti-embellished subway tunnels of my childhood.

This man wasn't a junkie. He was a traveling salesman with a thirst for good tequila and a love for women. (Those same thirsts were the downfall of our marriage.) He had plans—travel plans, plans for the future, plans for his son. He wasn't a junkie! His longest relationship was with his friend Miller Lite. Was alcohol even a problem or was it just my reaction to it? How do you know?

There was no alcohol in my house growing up, with the exception of a bottle of Manischewitz wine perched on a high shelf in our pantry. It was so infrequently used that the bottle had a thin layer of dust covering it. It was one of the most intriguing items in our home, along with the Lowenbrau beer dartboard in my father's basement woodshop. My parents never drank. In fact, my father claimed it made his nose run. I remember seeing my mom drink some wine at a Bar Mitzvah once, but she would otherwise say that alcohol might interfere with her medicines. There were prescription drugs to fix things beyond the common cold. Doctors were smarter than we were. We had doctors for anxiety, weight loss, and everything else you can think of.

I was supposed to be a Dr. Spock baby—that was my mother's plan. Before Dr. Spock's book, parents were told to let their baby cry and not indulge them, as that would spoil them and make them weak. If parents were uncomfortable with the rules, they were told that doctors knew best and should follow these instructions anyway.

Dr. Spock was revolutionary; he told parents to show their babies love and follow their instincts. This was the perfect plan for parents of an only child who wanted to devote their undivided attention to that one child. Dr. Spock was a controversial figure of sorts, having been held somewhat responsible for the unruly, anti-government youth of the 1960s. His gentle approach to parenting was accountable for that wild generation.

When my mother wasn't getting enough sleep, she quickly tossed the good doctor's paperback and decided to favor an old school doctor's advice. Dr. Emmett Holt instructed parents to let their child "cry it out." I think I remember crying so much for the first three years of my life that I grew tired of crying. This could be why it's so hard for me to cry today. I would wail and scream, holding on to the crib rail to no avail. I was alone in my screaming, a misplaced, blonde, alien being.

Growing up, I felt different for as long as I can remember. Like many kids of my generation, *Sesame Street* was our babysitter. Growing up in Teaneck, Susan and Bob were our real-life neighbors. We would regularly see them in Pathmark, our neighborhood supermarket. Somehow, this didn't take the mystery out of *Sesame Street*, and in my mind it was not far from that bus station over the George Washington Bridge. Maybe someday I could walk there with my mom.

"One of These Things" was my favorite song—the segments featuring it included Bob or Susan with four boxed items. Of those four there would be something out of place—three things you could eat (an apple, a hamburger, an ice cream cone) and one that was out of place (a random mitten). That was me—a random mitten. On walks to the bus stop with my mom, neighbors would always comment on my looks, as if they were confused. They'd say things like, "Look at her blue eyes," or "Where did she get such pretty blonde hair?" I never heard anyone say, "You look like your mom."

I knew before the private investigator called that my ex-husband wasn't alone when he died, but there were just so many unanswered questions. I'll never forget the call the night they found him.

My producer was holding my phone before we rolled. The phone rang, and he yelled across the crowded cocktail party from behind the camera, "Your phone is ringing again. Someone's calling you from Charlotte."

I told him to silence it. The cameras rolled, and flashbulbs flashed. It was a favorite party to cover every year. The Winterfest White Party was one of the best parties of the whole season. I smiled big in my white cocktail dress as I interviewed a favorite, the "Stud of the Sea," Captain Harold Lee Rosbach, the polished salty dog from the Bravo television hit, *Below Deck*.

Afterward, I walked off the red-carpet to several missed calls and a cryptic message from a Detective Collins: "This is Detective Collins. I am calling about your husband."

I immediately fell apart. It was an ugly moment of screaming, cursing, and pacing. There was no regard for anyone within my space—I went blank. *How could he get on a plane and never come back? Move quickly. Keep moving.* I laid on the ground in a heap waiting for the valet to pull up with my car.

As I cleaned, I thought about how crazy it was that I was answering a call from his kitchen. I looked at the tall, white cabinets with crown molding that I adored when we first bought the house. My eyes shifted to the sparkling, blue pool water, visible from the window, flanked by the custom-built Tiki Bar that a local Native American craftsman built for him.

"Would you believe I stayed in room 331 last night?" the private investigator said. He had died in room 332, just next-door. I felt like I could picture it in my head—where the bed was and where he collapsed.

I knew the room number from the homicide investigation report. Even on the night it happened, I felt like I could see the scene. It was like a movie that played out in my head. There were so many strange coincidences. I had so many questions. I wondered what events led up to his fate.

"Did you track her down? Is she willing to meet up with you?" I asked.

"Yes," he said, "I am meeting her at Starbucks later."

She was the stripper I had tracked down on Instagram who was with him on that fateful night—a dark-haired twenty-something about the same age as one of my daughters. *Not his usual type,* I thought, as I scrolled the images on her feed. *He liked blondes and big boobs.* This girl was cute, dark-haired, and tattooed. She had an edgy look; she was the kind of girl who is visibly rebellious. It was hard for me to wrap my head around her being the person who was with him when he died.

She responded within minutes to my direct message on Instagram, and soon called my number. *Maybe she needs to get this off her chest,* I thought. Of course, I wanted her to tell me how things went down. I imagined her running out of the room scared when he passed out. It must have been awful to find out later that he was dead. This was the thought that I manufactured in my head.

I was surprised to hear a different story.

She explained how happy she was that I reached out, that she thought about him every day (so did I). She went on to say how glad she had been when she saw him from the stage that night. He was standing at the bar with his tequila. "He wasn't a dance guy," she said.

I knew this. I knew everything about him—at least I did six years ago.

"I was excited to see him. He was so nice," she said and explained that they had met a few times when he would come into the bar. He would buy tequila for her and any other girls who caught his eye. He engaged everyone at the bar in lively conversation—Nick was always the life of the party and a real talent for entertaining multiple women. That was my big, stupid Italian.

She said she walked away to "work the room." He was strictly interested in tequila-fueled conversations and girls gathering at his throne at the bar. (After all, she needed to make money, and he wasn't taking her to the champagne room.) When he came in, he was a welcome distraction from the routine tasks of her employment.

When she was called up to the stage, she saw him talking to another girl, a blonde, Eastern European. I remembered this term—a "vulture" is strip club slang for a girl who isn't a team player. She operates solo in the club and has no respect for others. She's the kind who will poach a customer from another girl when they are called up to the stage. The girl I was talking to told me the next time she looked towards the bar, he was gone. She remembered thinking it was strange that he didn't say goodbye. As odd as it seemed, I found her relatable.

In the late 1990s, there was a new type of dance club. The gentleman's clubs in New York City had removed the illicitness from club culture. These high-end clubs became a hot spot of nightlife.

In my twenties, I worked as a cocktail waitress in one such club. Years before, as a young girl of eighteen on that cedar-lined street in Teaneck, I dreamed of the disco. I watched my childhood best friends' sisters feather their hair to Farrah Fawcett-perfection as their boyfriends picked them up in shiny gold Firebirds with actual birds painted on the hoods. Gold cars and the gold lame gowns were my style, and I would dance at Studio 54 when I grew up.

The next afternoon, hotel management finally went into the room after he didn't check out and ignored their knocks on the door. When they found his body, the dancer's phone was also found. It was an older iPhone with a cracked screen and sparkling case. She said she had used the "find my iPhone" app to trace it back to the hotel and explained that was why she was spotted in the lobby. She also explained everything else in detail, including how she filed a police report for the stolen phone. She wasn't hiding anything and went to the hotel lobby with the police in tow. She had never been at the hotel before; she wouldn't know where the room was. She left the hotel lobby without retrieving it and got ready for her next shift without a phone.

Later that day, the police questioned her. They did just what was required. When they assessed the scene, they knew what they had in front of them. To them, he was just another fentanyl case to add to the staggering number of deaths in North Carolina in late 2018.

To me, however, this wasn't just another overdose.

"The reason I'm a Nixonite is because of his indestructibility and resilience. Nixon never quit."
—*Roger Stone*

Chapter 6

Pushed onto the Tracks

J knew they would come after me. They wanted to silence me and destroy everything I had worked for—my career and my public persona.

I had been trying to make a difference. I was fighting against their injustice, abuse, lack of regard for human dignity. This wasn't a partisan issue—it was a human issue. There was nothing political about it; that was my own naïve belief.

It was not only horrible to watch my mother's decline, it was even uglier observing their tactics, from the overmedicating of patients to the lack of staff presence. The nursing home didn't really seem to care about patients; it seemed to only care about profits.

In the beginning, however, it was different. The facility was intimate and seemed homey. We were greeted by a woman with a heavy Finnish accent who offered us a cup of tea on arrival. There was the smell of fresh-baked bread and a petite nurse pushing a cart with small plates for the residents.

At first, I was concerned. I remembered history lessons with my father and knew that Finland was an ally of Nazi Germany. It hoped to regain the territory it lost to Russia. It also had a minuscule Jewish population of Russian Jews before the war.

Refugees came into Finland from Germany in the 1930s, but most were only passing through. Unlike the other German-occupied countries and allies, Finland was different; it was never asked to turn over its Jews. Finland was a strange ally; Finnish Jews fought on the front alongside the Germans, and no one saw this as a problem. Only some Jewish refugees were deported with a larger group of Latvian and Russian "undesirables." It wasn't even clear if they were deported because of their religious affiliation.

My father's love of history made me think that he would have liked this facility for my mom. At this point, she wasn't going to the temple or interested in religion. The Finnish woman was nice, and she seemed to care, but the sunshine, rainbows, and cups of tea were fleeting. I began waking up to the reality that my mom was just another body in a wheelchair that needed to be dealt with.

After the introduction of a new director, things began to change. This person's former facility made headlines when its patients suffered heatstroke during a hurricane and subsequent loss of power. It was soon clear this new addition was not there to be anything more than a figurehead, and the home's focus became greed without regard.

The halls felt more stoic; the dayroom seemed darker. The eyes of the patients were emptier; the clouds had rolled in. You felt the chill—not in temperature but emotion. The place had become cold and callous.

I knew they had it out for me, for I might be the one to expose them. They were afraid that I would call the press. I might gather my twenty years of connections to elevate the public narrative on neglect.

At the time, this wasn't even on my radar. I wasn't concerned about my soapbox, I was only worried about my mom. I was selfish, perhaps, as an only child that was living in their bubble. I was not thinking about others. Not yet at least.

I hadn't considered going to press, but I felt the fear. I wasn't prepared for how far they would go. I didn't know the nursing home, lawyers, and professional guardians were all in the same pool together, swimming around. It was an incestuous orgy of ugly people. Picture a scene so disturbing you would never want to walk into it, and if you happened to catch a glimpse of it, it would be burned into your brain for life. Theirs was a hideous expression of the human form; the apparent conflicts were hard to fathom.

"That's why we chose the red berets, to stand out in a crowd like lollipops," Curtis Sliwa of the Guardian Angels said in 1979. The idea was to create a uniformed, visible presence. The Angels were like soldiers safeguarding the subway. They avoided confrontations and violence whenever possible. They were there merely to report crimes, intervene for the innocent, and act as witnesses. Sometimes, they'd make a citizen's arrest by holding a suspect captive until law enforcement could take over.

After my favorite Yankee had passed, my dad took me to another ball game at the stadium. He had season tickets through his company, and many times, a big group from his work would go. This was one of those days and one of those games. We would take the train to the Bronx and meet him there with the guys from work.

That summer, I also had convinced my mom to let me take dance classes in New York. Taking classes there was a better option than taking classes in Teaneck. Carole Naso's Dance Academy was great for suburban kids, but I wanted to have a city girl edge. Manhattan just seemed more competitive, more professional, and was bound to lead to something more substantial. My mom found an instructor uptown at the 92nd Street YWHA, which was a short ride downtown.

I packed a small rectangular TWA bag that my grandmother brought back on one of her recent trips. I was on a plane only once, and I was a baby at the time. I imagined that it was luxurious; the stewardesses dressed in crisp, pretty uniforms with perfectly tied scarfs and cute hats. The airliner would have comfortable seats, cold beverages and little bags of salted nuts. There was no need to keep moving like we had to do on the subway. No one was strung out on drugs laying in the terminal. Air travel was a safe, relaxing, and comfortable way. There was no danger.

My bag was packed with well-worn ballet shoes, a new pink leotard, and black, footless tights. (They were specific about the uniform in dance class.)

Ballet dancing had rules, discipline, and structure; it was predictable. As an aspiring dancer, my build was perfect for it. I was petite, with long arms and legs, and skinny. My figure was very different than my mother's—she was always struggling with her weight.

It was the last class of the summer, before the school year started right after Labor Day. A dance class on the Upper East Side would no longer be practical—during the school year, I'd have to settle for the suburban classes with my friends.

That particular morning was like the others that summer. The alarm clock went off, and I got mom up. I made her tea and got her some toast. I had her pillbox with her medicine waiting on the dining room table—she couldn't risk a headache on a day like this. There wouldn't be time for a nap if she didn't feel well in the afternoon.

After class, we rode the IRT #4 train from Lexington Avenue, which had recently assigned the color green to the number. This train was akin to the B that ran uptown to the Bronx and downtown to Brooklyn. Its green reminded me that—besides the concrete that dominated the landscape—there were botanical gardens in the Bronx. This oasis was set in an area riddled with crime and poverty and showed that amid chaos, there was a sanctuary.

My favorite part of the garden was the enormous fountain in front of the library, which featured a scene that seemed unexpectedly heroic—a feminine-looking, petite sea nymph rode a pair of majestic seahorses aided by two cherubs, barreling through the crest of a wave. In the underworld of the pool below, two visibly scared and startled creatures, a mermaid and merman, were scattering. These fishtailed freaks didn't notice the nymph approaching until she was almost on top of them. They had to hurry to avoid being run over by the oncoming chariot. It was a magical scene.

My father, with his love of factual history, would remind me that art wasn't the only part of the garden that was magical. Science was also empowering, and the real work was done behind the scenes in this oasis. There would be no Rice Krispies for breakfast had Alexander Pierce Anderson not invented puffed rice as a botanist working at the New York Botanical Garden. America's greatest inventor, Thomas Edison, also created there, developing rubber tires made from goldenrod plants.

As we boarded the IRT to meet my father, I saw them—four red berets. They were young men, maybe eighteen or twenty, at best. Without their uniforms, they would have looked like regular teens in the area. On a train that had been dubbed the "muggers express," the year before, there would be no need to keep moving between cares today. They were here, and we were safe.

Earlier that summer, my mother's subway fears had been realized in all the New York City papers' headlines. A seventeen-year-old girl suffered a severed right hand. Witnesses said a mugger pushed her in front of an oncoming train.

Renee Katz was a senior at the High School of Music and Art. She was attacked in broad daylight on her way to school. After she was pushed, she had rolled to her left and was screaming for her mother as the train approached. She was still conscious as the train pinned her between the second car and the platform overhang. The police retrieved her severed hand from between the tracks after the train was removed from the station.

There was a sense of tranquility as we sat, side by side that afternoon on our plastic seats; seating was rare on a trip to the stadium. We were late when our train rolled into the Bronx onto an elevated platform—the game was already into a few innings.

The metal doors creaked open, and our calm was broken. The red berets rushed into action. In front of the first car, an elderly man was lying crumpled on the tracks. His shopping bags were strewn on the platform and ground below. The contents of the shopping bags were thrown about with noticeable force. The train was at a full stop when someone had pushed the old man onto the tracks, and his attacker was escaping to the nearby stairwell that led down to the street. Something made me run in the same direction. I had zero awareness of where my mom was and no consideration for danger in front of me.

We were in the middle of a fight—there was screaming and anger. My adrenaline was pumping. One of the Guardian Angels bolted ahead of the first car to aid the man, leaping onto the tracks below. The other three were racing towards the stairs, just feet away.

I could hear the altercation before I saw it. It was the sound of the Guardians kicking the living shit out of the perpetrator. It was that "boom-pow" of a *Batman* cartoon as their use of martial arts took the bad guy to the ground. He surrendered, begging them to stop. The smallest of the Angels tackled him. He was face down and not moving.

The Guardian Angels were real-life superheroes. They had jumped into danger, to save this fragile, old man that they didn't even know.

When they proposed a guardian for my mother, I embraced the idea. I wanted an advocate for her. I wanted a hero—someone to fight with me against the sub-standard practices of this nursing home. I wanted someone who would swoop in and save the day. I expected this person, much like the Angels on that Bronx platform, would lift my mother off of the tracks and save her from the train that was headed her way.

Little did I know this guardian was just another fishtailed freak swimming in the incestuous pool of the underworld.

"I'm a fast healer. I was on the air a week after I got shot."
—*Curtis Sliwa, founder of the Guardian Angels*

Chapter 7 ——————

The Bearded Man

𝕴 was in therapy from the time I was three; it was my mother's idea of being proactive. She thought you should see a doctor before you have a problem because you will inevitably have one.

I kept waiting to figure out what was wrong with me. In some ways, I'm still waiting.

Dr. Spady would take me for ice cream, or we would play dolls in her office. By the time I was seven or eight, I was utterly bored with the whole process. I felt like there was little purpose in our conversations about my week at school or my latest favorite song. However, this schedule wasn't under my control. On Tuesdays, every week, I went to therapy.

My uncle was a psychiatrist. He was married to my stylish, hip aunt on Long Island. He seemed to be critical of everything, especially my mother. Her love for doctors made her susceptible to his probing and sometimes inappropriate questions. I was not too fond of his conversation skills, as he seemed intent on analyzing every answer for a diagnosis. This probably unfairly biased my opinion towards my own therapist.

After my appointment, we would jump off the bus in front of Miller's pharmacy, where my mother would pick up medicine, and I might get a candy bar. There were inevitably errands to run and shopping to do. This was the only part of the day that mattered to me. Knowing that I was always reluctant to go, my mom would always make up for it afterward with post-appointment shopping.

We took the bus to our downtown shopping area of Cedar Lane. There was a one-mile stretch of storefronts with everything from Kosher restaurants to stationery shops, pharmacies, and a movie theatre. There was also County Discount, a store that had everything a five and dime offered, such as toys, hair ribbons, and flip flops.

There was also a record store, which was my favorite place to go. My love of music had advanced to using my allowance money to buy an LP or single. Sometimes, I would even practice my negotiating skills with my mother, as I often talked her into purchasing another album for me ahead of the following week's allowance. Billy Joel, Donna Summer, and the *Grease* soundtrack dominated my collection. The walk back to our house always felt more fulfilling with packages, like there had been an accomplishment at the end of the work-filled day.

I knew there had been an incident in my mother's past—an actual mugging. I imagined it as if it was me as if it was my story; she had told it to me so many times. I could picture it.

Brooklyn was not that different from a town in New Jersey. I knew the neighborhood because it was close to where my grandmother lived, across from Sheepshead Bay and near the beach. Manhattan Beach was another suburb dominated by a minority—Jews like us. My mom had attended the Yeshiva there and went on to James Madison High School. It was a neighborhood full of families and small, tightly-spaced houses, with a few apartment buildings scattered in between.

My mother, a twelve-year-old on her way to a friend's birthday party, was walking on West End Avenue to Oriental Boulevard when a bearded white man in his forties approached her. He was far from intimidating in his dress and stature, but was a little unkempt, with his plaid shirt half tucked in. He seemed kind and vulnerable. He also stuck out to her because he didn't seem to be of the same ethnicity as the rest of the neighborhood—she immediately sensed that he wasn't Jewish.

The man was visibly nervous and distraught. He told her that he had lost his twin daughters. They had been shopping together, and they simply vanished. He didn't know the neighborhood and asked if she could help him for just a few minutes because she was about their age and would know where to look. He assured her it wouldn't take very long.

My mother was a trusting girl who wanted to be polite. She left the birthday present that she had been carrying with a shopkeeper and headed out with the man. They walked up and down the street, calling the girls' names. They ran up and down driveways, checked alleyways, and walked briskly past the stores and other pedestrians. They asked others if they had seen the red-headed twins. Maybe they had headed for the beach, which wasn't far away, or went to the park near Oriental Boulevard.

As my mom led the way, she began to question her instincts about the stranger, but felt a pang of guilt as she became unsure of his motives and story. She shrugged it off, and they continued to walk together. She began making excuses about how late she was for the party and how she had to go. Each time, he would reassure her, telling her he was confident that they would find them quickly with her help. Without her, he would be lost and may never locate them.

As they approached the park, my mom said she became less nervous—perhaps this was the calm before the storm. She continued to shrug off her instincts and invested herself in helping this innocent, bearded man.

Before they got to the beach, there was a brick structure containing public restrooms and a storage shed for the park. As they approached, he asked her to check the ladies' room. They separated, and he checked the men's room.

My mother checked each stall but found nothing. Afterward they met outside. She could have trusted her gut and run away right then, but she didn't. She was committed to helping, to doing the right thing. She disregarded that little voice inside. They walked around the large brick structure toward the back of the brick building with my mom leading the way. Maybe they were hiding in the storage shed, the one that the park workers didn't lock. My mom opened the door, and from behind, and the bearded man pushed her inside.

I remember the darkness descending when things began to change for her at the facility. A new presence had disrupted the lovely accents and helpful workers. There had been some things we had fought for at the home; overall, staff had listened to our concerns. Now those same concerns fell on deaf ears. The smiles of the workers had faded, and the residents seemed to lack the same level of contentment.

Brian, my mother's music therapist, spent mornings at the facility. Even when my mom couldn't put her thoughts together, she loved to sing. Music opened up the connections in her brain and wove her thoughts together in a way that made sense.

Brian called my phone after a visit and told me that my mom had a new favorite song. Together, while he strummed his guitar, they would sing "Take Me Home, Country Roads" by John Denver. A song about the Blue Ridge Mountains and West Virginia was an odd choice—Apparently my mom told him that it was one of her favorite "folk" songs.

As soon as he said, "folk song," I knew she was not fabricating a memory and that the song had not been Brian's choice. He explained that my mom had chosen to write new lyrics to it that morning. In his usual creative fashion, he went along with it. She created a song about going home to grass-covered roads in Brooklyn.

Brian was a significant departure from the norm at the facility—he was always a welcome face. He was even more welcome than her regular aide, who had been with my mom for a few years. She seemed to be growing frustrated with her decline and taking advantage of her failing ability to keep track of who was coming and going. She was helping other residents in the facility and not showing up as scheduled. Items of my mother's were also missing. Her old neighbors called, saying they had spotted my "mom's girl" with someone over at her prior facility. These sightings clarified that she had a side hustle.

Meanwhile, my mom was just adorable with Brian. She would often comment about how her boyfriend would be coming back to sing to her. These were bright spots in her failing mind and inability to make the same connections that she did years before. She was happy in those moments. When I think of her, I always go back to how peaceful and happy she was with Brian. She was singing, sharing stories from the past, and talking about Clarke Gable or her favorite movies.

In those days, she also knew me, knew my kids and was able to carry on a conversation. I realized this seemingly skilled facility was the only place she could be. After her discharge from the hospital and a possible mini stroke, my mom couldn't walk without assistance; she needed help in the bathroom and just about everywhere else. She would often forget she that couldn't walk and would try to get up from the wheelchair. She needed constant attention. I was doing the best I could, juggling my work schedule with daily visits and bringing in Brian, hiring another aide, and sending my adult daughters over to visit.

It was becoming tumultuous and unstable quickly. Gone were the pleasant Finnish accents and warm smiles. Now there were whispers, and my mom was afraid. It was hard to tell if these were fabrications of her mind. Were these old memories? How could she define them?

When I arrived, she would always be anxious to talk to me alone. She would immediately insist that we leave the day room with the others. She would want to go outside to the courtyard, under the arbor, where we were outside of earshot. She would grab my arm and lean in. She would tell me in terrifying detail about the man with the beard.

Inside the storage shed, he pushed her against a wall with the force of his brawny stature. His shirt and clothing were becoming more disheveled as he physically attacked her. He brandished a knife and covered her mouth so that she couldn't scream. He cut her arm, drawing blood to show her he wasn't afraid to hurt her. She was so scared of the blood and pain that she was unable to move.

He used a rope to tie her hands behind her back and told her he would uncover her mouth if she would succumb to him and promised not to scream. She begged him to let her go, prayed for her life, and pleaded with him not to kill her. His personality had shifted from the nice man on the street—his soul was gone, turned off like a light switch. She was unable to fight back.

Now, outside of the facility, safe from the others who could hear her, my mom spoke of the bearded man. She told me that he was in the here and now: "He keeps coming back—he's here almost every day. He's sometimes in my room." She was terrified and said he was a "robber." She was positive he had come for her. She wasn't safe, and her wheelchair prevented her from moving.

I reassured her that she would be safe, and there were guardian angels protecting her. No one would allow the bearded man to hurt her. I promised over and over again.

"Fear does the choosing between right and wrong."
—John Denver

Chapter 8 ────────────

Identity Crisis

1979 into 1980 was a turning point; it was only the end of a decade but the beginning of a cultural shift for America. There was change back to conservatism.

Amidst the pop culture, and Rod Stewart asking, "Do Ya Think I'm Sexy?" there was an energy crisis and gas lines. There was political discourse, and a lack of trust in our Government. The Ayatollah Khomeini, who had returned to Iran to establish an Islamic Republic, was hostile to American interests and influence. Inflation was on the rise, and various parts of the United States were experiencing energy shortages.

The Plymouth Valiant sat in those gas lines many times. President Jimmy Carter argued the oil crisis was "the moral equivalent of war." His ability to deal with international relations was in question, as critics said his proposals would make the situation worse, not better.

In November 1979, revolutionaries seized the American Embassy in Iran, and Carter imposed an embargo against Iranian oil. He was given a short opportunity for political redemption when the Khomeini regime caught public attention by taking American hostages, who were a group of students and militants.

For a moment, Carter's calm approach toward the crisis bumped up his approval ratings—this was referred to as a "rally round the flag" effect. Later that year, he would address the nation in a televised speech about the "crisis of confidence" in America; this came to be known as his "national malaise" speech. Carter's reactions fueled the mentality of crisis. On the other hand, there was an optimism from his opposition, Ronald Reagan. Reagan's supporters praised him for running a positive and upbeat campaign.

This was the summer that I knew another reason I was different from my parents. I knew, with 100 percent certainty, that I was a conservative Republican.

The election of 1980 was in many ways a parallel to the election of 2016. Reagan promised a restoration of the nation's military strength. He wanted to end the empty campaign promises and the "trust me" government that was failing the American people. He pledged to restore economic health, which seemed to be a logical way to solve the problems the country was facing. He wanted to end inflation and promised a balanced budget within three years. This would accompany a 30 percent reduction in tax rates over those same years. Concerning the economy, Reagan famously said, "A recession is when your neighbor loses his job. A depression is when you lose yours. And recovery is when Jimmy Carter loses his."

Reagan also criticized the "windfall profit tax" that Carter and Congress enacted that year. It impacted domestic oil production, and he promised to repeal it as president. The tax was not a tax on profits, but a tax on the difference between the price control-mandated and market prices.

By April 1980, the public's opinions had shifted even further to the right. Carter took the blame for the Iran hostage crisis and a failed rescue attempt. The followers of the Ayatollah Khomeini burned American flags and chanted anti-American slogans. The captors brazenly paraded American hostages in public.

Critics saw Carter as an inept leader who had failed to solve economic problems at home. Internationally, he was degrading our power by showing our weaknesses to terrorists. His supporters defended the president as a decent, well-intentioned man, who was unfairly criticized for problems out of his control that had been escalating for years. Surprisingly, my parents were those people.

Central Park was another oasis set in the middle of the concrete jungle. There were playgrounds peppered throughout and adventures to be had. Every time you ventured into the park there was something you hadn't seen before—a new path, a new playground, horses, and even a carousel.

One of our favorite spots was the Central Park Zoo. It was near Museum Row and close to everything you would need for a leisurely cultural experience in New York City.

We met my maternal aunt on that spring day; she was visiting her psychiatrist husband at work. My cousins weren't with her, so it would just be the three of us. My mom's older sister later succumbed to the degenerative brain ailments that took away my grandmother and my mom. But on that day, she was a hip mom in her late 40s wearing crisp white slacks, a pretty silk blouse, and gold-trimmed loafers.

She and her husband lived on Long Island. They were upper middle class Jews. Great Neck was much like Teaneck, with an overwhelming population of Jews compared to other demographics scattered throughout towns and villages in the tri-state area. We walked and talked that afternoon in the park. It was a beautiful day with my classy aunt. We lunched at Tavern on the Green, which was the epitome of class. The light inside was pure sunshine, like a beautiful old brick building with a greenhouse attached. The expansive walls of glass let the outside in as waiters bustled about in white tuxedos.

I was wholly convinced that I saw Farrah Fawcett at a nearby table. She was with two men with wide, loose ties who had tossed their suit jackets aside and rolled up their sleeves. They looked like they were engaged in a meaningful conversation, exchanging papers across the table. I imagined that they might be Hollywood movie producers. As we exited, a cameraman sat outside, lying in wait for his next paparazzi moment. Farrah flashed that wide, white smile, and I knew it was her. She was blonde, thin, polished, and tanned. She had that Hollywood look, but she was different than many of the celebrities of the day. Farrah was clean-cut—not a part of the generation's drug culture. She seemed more interested in playing tennis and was all-American. She was on television, and I wanted to be on television.

I questioned my lack of chutzpah. What if I had said hello? Would that have been a life-altering moment? My brush with a celebrity. Someone who could have been a real role model or mentor to a young lady like me. Farrah wasn't my first celebrity sighting, but she was different. Growing up in the shadow of Manhattan gave you an understanding that celebrities were people just like us. I was running into the stars of *Sesame Street* as a young girl, and I knew that John Travolta grew up just one town over in Englewood.

Travolta played Vinnie Barbarino in *Welcome Back, Kotter*, before moving on to movie superstardom in *Saturday Night Fever* and *Grease*. Brooke Shields, who was not much older than me, lived in nearby Haworth and went to my dentist. There were also the people behind the scenes—the producers, directors, writers, and journalists. Many kids had parents with these cool jobs and their associated perks. These were access to concerts, tickets, and plays. There were exciting parties and events. I saw it, I envied it, and I wanted it too.

We descended through the pathways and headed across the park to the zoo. We stopped along the way, and my mom and aunt would chat. As they did, I would climb the exposed bedrock that stuck out all over the park. Beyond the climbing stones were massive skyscrapers that lined the park. Each building was unique—there were modern glass structures, classic, and Gothic and neo-Gothic with gargoyles perched at their tops warding off the evil from the skies and sin that lurked below on the streets.

Near the zoo, the energy was always infectious. This was my favorite spot. The massive clock chimed above the brick archway between the Central Park Zoo and the Tisch Children's Zoo. The whimsical George Delacorte Musical Clock was a statuesque play on a cuckoo clock. Its donor, George T. Delacorte, was a fan of the medieval mechanical clocks found in European squares. In perfect time, every half an hour, a band of bronze animal sculptures came to life and played a repertoire of children's songs to the delight of the guests below the arches.

There were always vendors near those arches with pinwheels and plastic bird flutes that you would fill with a bit of water to make them sing like songbirds. There was also a larger item that I always had my eyes set on—marionettes. They were a pricy item at twenty dollars. I imagined that I would be a master of puppetry like one of the von Trapp children in my mom's favorite movie, *The Sound of Music.*

Some were animals reminiscent of those in the clock above. There was a bear, a goat, a kangaroo, a penguin, a hippo and some monkeys. There was also an elephant, a donkey, a mouse, and a peanut. Today, I hoped that having the third-party witness to my negotiation might help my cause. I was successful—my puppet dream would finally happen! It came with a caveat of sorts—I would settle for the peanut. I knew this was a nod to my mother's candidate, our current president, Jimmy Carter. For the love of puppets, I acquiesced—the puppet purchase was a defining moment.

For the next year, international tensions grew, and the country's economic slide continued. I played with the peanut somewhat reluctantly until the strings become entangled. They eventually rendered the puppet powerless.

I was sure that Jimmy Carter was not the candidate I would back, but I was too young to vote. I spent a good deal of time trying to persuade my parents that they needed to switch parties. They were amused and used me as a sideshow act to entertain their friends and our family.

It all seemed so logical, just like it does today. I was only an elementary school student, but it only took an elementary education to figure out what was wrong with politics in America. I did listen to my father—we read the newspapers together and watched the nightly news. His thoughts on Reagan led me to believe that he was in denial about his own political identity. It was clear that he had a valid fear from escaping the Nazi occupation, and this was a fear that certainly Reagan saw. They both understood that Americans were slowly but surely losing their freedoms. He had an intellectual conviction and a passion to make a change. This was during the height of boisterous calls for political liberalism, much like today.

Reagan was a recovering liberal Democrat. Like Trump, we had a president who switched parties as his perspective on America shifted with the party's change. As a young man, he was a huge Roosevelt supporter and took part in his first presidential campaign by making speeches for Harry Truman. As a man in his twenties in Hollywood, he saw sophistication in politics through rose-colored glasses. By 1964, Reagan was in for Goldwater and thought the conservatives were on the right side of things. He took off the rose-colored glasses and saw clearly and logically. He went against the grain by becoming a conservative. It was a bold move and not fashionable among the Hollywood elite.

In his presidential campaign of 1980, Reagan focused on bringing people together to build a better America. He attacked his opponents and pointed out their weaknesses. He called his opponent's plan a "crazy quilt" of election-year promises that would likely fall apart in the wash after the election.

The Democrats played these like shell game and regularly mocked Reagan as a dangerous cowboy. He took a stand against international threats with fiery speeches and never wavered in confronting the Soviet Union.

In retrospect, it was clear that Reagan was precisely the antidote to Democratic political establishment of the 1970s. He would not be satisfied with merely managing the Soviet peril—he was determined to triumph over it, like President Trump over China.

Ronald Reagan got elected president in 1980 by posing a simple question to American voters: "Are you better off than you were four years ago?" Americans were fed up; they were tired of the status quo of politics. Like Trump, Reagan won the presidency as a maverick outsider who was willing to take on the Washington status quo.

Trump's 2016 victory was laid out by the Tea Party before it was backed by a more sweeping majority of America. In the 1960s, the Goldwater movement pushed forward the political insurgency that culminated in Reagan's 1980 victory.

President Reagan was under attack by the elder statesman of the Democratic Party. Clark Clifford disparaged the new president as a "dunce." That "dunce" became a man revered by America. He defeated the scourge of communism and had an unwavering moral and political clarity. He bucked the conventional politics of the day and welcomed the challenge of the opposition.

Ronald Reagan referred to the nation's condition in 1980 as a "human tragedy." From where I walked in my red sandals, as an elementary school student, this seemed very accurate. Under the streets of New York City, there were subway tunnels filled with crime and despair. We were waiting in traffic and the gas lines. There was evidence of failing policy and a failing country. Career politicians did not have the interests of my family or me on their minds. This was factual and undebatable.

Reagan said things that made me feel empowered and united to something bigger. He said we were part of the fabric of America; we were all in this together. One of his tag lines was so good that it was recently repurposed. That tagline was "Make America Great Again."

"While I take inspiration from the past, like most Americans, I live for the future."
—Ronald Reagan

Chapter 9 ────────────────────────────

Witch Hunt

During periods of media frenzy, I get most of my work done in the morning between 3:00 and 4:00 a.m. When things are quiet, I can focus outside of my normal type-A brain functions. Early in the morning, I am more targeted than my high energy, spinning, mid-day mind.

In folklore, this time is the "witching hour" or "devil's hour," and it is most associated with supernatural events. Ghosts and demons are thought to appear and be at their most potent. This activity is believed by some in Western Christianity to be spurred in the absence of prayer during this early morning period. In the days of the Salem witch trials, women caught outside without sufficient reason during this time were sometimes executed on suspicion of practicing the craft. The government prosecuted more than 200 people accused of witchcraft in colonial Massachusetts. Of those, thirty were found guilty, and nineteen were executed. It was a time when any accusation was an offense against the government, and it was the deadliest witch hunt in Colonial America.

In reality, it was a notorious case of mass hysteria spurred by fake news stories. One of the men, Giles Corey, was pressed to death for refusing to enter a plea of guilty or not guilty. The magistrate needed a conviction and wanted to send a message to others by imposing torture.

Corey was a dedicated church member but was widely known as a stubborn man. After his arrest, he was subjected to pressing in an attempt to force him to plead. According to the law at the time, a person who refused to plead could not be tried. "Pressing" someone wasn't pressing them through a verbal interrogation—it meant that the person was stripped naked with boards placed on their body. These were topped off with heavy boulders. Lawmakers would give the prisoner three morsels of stale bread and a few drops of water each day. This torture continued until the individual died or was willing to plea.

Giles's tongue was pressed out of his mouth. The sheriff used a cane to push it back in. Corey was asked three times to enter a plea, but each time bravely he cried out, "More weight." Most people would have given in when accused of a crime by the government.

About thirty years before the trials, a man named Joseph Glanvill said that he could prove that a supernatural realm existed. He reasoned that the magical world could not be denied by those who believed in God; if you held this belief, you must maintain that angels and demons are also part of the supernatural realm.

I went to Salem with my parents in 1982. My mother was concerned that adventure might be too scary, but I was hoping that we would encounter a spirit. She suggested that perhaps we should go when I was older, but I persisted—after all, this was an educational experience in American history.

Perhaps, we would witness the apparition of Giles Corey. According to folklore, he acts as a harbinger, walking the graveyard where he's buried each time a disaster is about to strike. He didn't appear to us in 1982, which was a sign that there was no impending doom. If I had gone back to Salem in 2018, maybe he would have warned me of the imminent disaster.

My work-related witching hours of these early mornings are usually focused on getting ahead of the next day of press. This is a supernatural feat. I channel my twenty years of career experience in media, utilize my well-honed predictive skills to stare into the future (to determine what they will report on next), and to advise a high-profile client in crisis. It's like a chess game, but you plot your next move with a crystal ball.

Crisis clients are the most exhilarating to work with because you know you are making a difference. I have skills beyond most in this business, and my confidence doesn't waver there. Before the 2016 election and on the surge of my on-air media work, these behind-the-headline media clients were mostly NFL players and celebrities. I handled PR and media as quietly as I could, sometimes intertwined with a law firm. These were cases typically related to family law disputes and getting ahead of press-reported problems ranging from domestic disputes caught on camera to drunken debauchery. It was a simpler time of working on getting the best possible outcome for a client when the tabloid papers came knocking.

After Hillary Clinton was defeated in 2016, life as I knew it changed. The war on conservatives began. The fires raged, fueled by the newspapers. Moreover, my client demographic shifted.

Now they were people more like me, conservatives targeted by a Democrat agenda.

The mainstream media were hellbent on making their pre-determined narrative fit the witch hunt. Television outlets were funded by George Soros, as a well-positioned extension of Democrat political campaigning. (The left doesn't mind the influence because they're the ones who benefit.)

George Soros is a typical billionaire. He's featured on "World's Richest Men" lists. He's smart and calculating but has a more sinister side. He discovered that he could buy opinions from financially struggling news outlets. (With the changes in the way America consumed news, there were lots of opportunities.) The cherry on top of the sundae was that he never needed to buy a single media outlet. Instead, he spawned several foundations with important sounding names to influence causes that he wanted to elevate, notably politics and policy. His goal is to further the Democrat agenda and support a globalist ideal.

Soros serves as the founder and chair of the Open Society Foundation. He has given away more than $32 billion of his fortune to fund it. The foundation supports liberal positions—big government and abortion, among them. It is also overwhelmingly anti-Israel. Its 2020 budget was $1.2 billion.

Through a pretty navigable maze, you can trace his ties to more than thirty mainstream news outlets, including: CNN, *The Washington Post*, *The New York Times*; and all the other usual suspects. During the 2004 election, he spent $27 million desperately trying to defeat George W. Bush. In 2016, he committed more than $25 million to support Hillary Clinton and other Democrat candidates and causes. Soros even bestowed a $1.8 million gift on National Public Radio (NPR), which jeopardized its federal funding. These donations and foundations are illustrative of the influence that his buying power has over the American news media and what they report.

Way before becoming the target of salacious newspaper headlines, I was behind them with my clients. Headlines are often twisted; often, they don't even reflect the contents of the article. They are created to capture your short attention span. The sexier the headline, the better.

Often, the writer responsible for the article doesn't control the published headline—that is determined by the editor. Those within the media work with the government to craft future headlines ahead of the story.

Andrew McCabe's book, *The Threat (How the FBI Protects America in The Age of Terror and Trump)*, hit bookstore shelves on February 19, 2019, just as the Russian collusion story was beginning to fizzle out. On page 212, he wove an imaginary story about China, a consultant advocating for its government, and an FBI investigation. However, the consultant in the book wasn't a real person.

Based on the timing, this narrative had all the elements the press was looking for. A few weeks later, they spun fiction into a reality as they turned their attention to my client, Cindy Yang.

The headlines were the epitome of "sex sells." New England Patriots owner Robert Kraft was busted for prostitution in a Palm Beach County, Florida strip mall sex spa. Most of America had the innocent perception that this was next to Trump's winter White House, Mar-a-Lago. Even better for the prostitution story was that he also happened to frequent Mar-a-Lago.

"An Asian massage parlor offering 'happy endings' and an NFL owner," said the story. A *New York Magazine* headline screamed, "How Cindy Yang Learned to Throw a Party at Mar-a-Lago." *The Palm Beach Post* wrote, "Trump selfie-queen Cindy

Yang ran unlicensed spa, illegal in Florida." "She Extols Trump, Guns and the Chinese Communist Party Line" was the direction of *The New York Times.*

I've lived in Palm Beach County for more than twenty years; I was engrained in its social scene. It only grew when like-minded Americans became passionate about supporting President Trump. Trump supporters were my people. Cindy stuck out—not only was she Asian, but she always had an infectious smile. She was one of those people who went out of their way to greet you as you approached. I didn't know her well, but we had exchanged pleasantries on a few occasions. She seemed like a sweet person. Her heavy accent made it a little challenging to communicate, but her smile made up for it.

She called one day, distraught; the panic in her voice made me stop in my tracks. "Why are they doing this?" she said. We met face to face, leaving our phones outside the room where we met. She was crying and shaking uncontrollably. The smile that was her signature had been erased. She was an intelligent immigrant woman, who came to this country to have a better life with her mom many years ago and who had done everything she could to build her American dream. She was broken and shattered.

Hers was a familiar story—Cindy came to this country for an opportunity she wasn't born into. She pursued an education, learned a new language, and became a citizen. She gained an interest in politics. She embraced capitalism and bought and sold several businesses. One of the businesses she sold was that infamous spa. In fact, she sold it seven years before the Kraft rub and tug debacle.

Yes, seven years before the story. The facts were insignificant, however. The press-generated narrative had been launched, and now it was time to use this as the latest story to discredit President

Trump and the people who support him. The most disturbing part about profiling of Cindy Yang in the media wasn't the sexual innuendos, it was the xenophobia.

Cindy is an immigrant and represents so many things that the left claims to embrace. To see her targeted in this way was utterly disgusting. Had she been an illegal immigrant who didn't support a Republican candidate, this would have never happened to her.

I flashed back to Andrew McCabe's book published just a few weeks earlier and realized that the media had only just begun to spin the story. It played out like an NFL play down on the field. The media's moves were pre-planned and calculated. It had a quarterback and the ability to carry the story down the field; it added other players, changing some out as it went. There was talk of an FBI investigation, predicted in the book that never materialized outside the media reports. There was also a Mar-a-Lago intruder, a Chinese female, who Cindy never met and did not know.

There was an overall desire to link my client to every other Asian person of questionable origin and motive. If they were Asian, then they must know Cindy Yang—it was racial profiling at its finest. *New York Magazine* asked me why I thought Cindy attended so many parties and posted so many pictures as if this was unique: "Who doesn't like to go to a party and take a selfie?" I responded. "I think we are all social climbing. That's bipartisan; it's a human thing. We are all looking to be the best versions of ourselves that we can. So now you [the press] are chastising people for wanting to make their lives better—by making better friends, going to better parties, and buying something nice for themselves."

I encourage my clients to speak up and face the press. Otherwise, they are destined to become a manufactured character, rather than a genuine person. They will be positioned the way the media chooses and will inevitably become dehumanized.

Cindy finally fought back by doing multiple interviews, back-to-back. Some of the better, more responsible journalists were interested in the backstory. Who was this mysterious Chinese woman? Why did she support President Trump? Was she a prostitute? Was she a spy? Was she working for a foreign government?

Cindy was direct and poised—she looked the interviewers in the eye. She made her point heard by saying that she had been targeted for her views and support for Trump. She hit home runs repeatedly with her truthful blurbs, saying that she was an easy target as she was a non-native English speaker, and she was a Chinese Republican and a proud American Citizen.

Her rise to the occasion was admirable and empowering. I watched her confidence as she addressed the interviewers with her heavy accent. She was on fire, but at the end of a very long day, she looked at me and said, "No more interviews." That fire had raged and quickly burned itself out.

The headlines had her burned at the stake. They had taken so much of her pride, embarrassed her, and hurt her family. I told *New York Magazine*: "I felt immediate empathy for Cindy." After everything that transpired for me in the months after, I empathized with her even more. Cindy wanted to fade into the background, but she faced her fears and stood up against the fake news at the moment.

"I never complied but prayed against the devil all my days. I will say it as if it were my last time. I am clear of this sin."
—Mary Eastey, transcript, Salem witch trials

Chapter 10 ———————

In March the Nazis

How could they keep leaving her like this? Slumped in a wheelchair, my mom was almost unresponsive. Her eyes twitched as she momentarily awakened. She was drooling on herself. Where were the nurses? Why was she alone at a table in the dining room with no one to feed her?

Coming into the facility to visit my mom was becoming more and more frustrating. She was getting worse; her steep decline was evident. Why wouldn't they listen to me? I was her daughter, her power of attorney, and her health care surrogate. Why weren't they including me in the care planning meeting? I begged them to take her off the medications that were sedating her. Didn't I have some say in the process? Wasn't the ombudsman supposed to work for families like ours? Did anyone even show up after I called and complained? What about the call I made to the Department of Children and Families? Was it another wasted rant? I was crying out with no one to listen to me. No one was coming. No one cared.

I saw the bearded man hurrying through the cafeteria; he pushed his way past the residents lined up by the door with little regard and marched his way into the kitchen. He was here, just like my mom had whispered. There was always truth in the things she said, even if they made little sense to me at that moment. The thought faded to more important things—I needed to feed my mom her dinner.

Historic recurrence is the repetition of similar events in history. *Historic replication* has been applied to the overall history of the world to repetitive events that bear a striking similarity. Recurrences take place due to ascertainable circumstances and chains of causality.

When my grandmother's Alzheimer's disease began to manifest, she was living in her apartment with an aide coming in to help. As things took a more serious turn, she couldn't be left alone. She was terrified of the people outside the door. The Nazis were still a vivid memory for her—she had fled Austria in 1938 with her husband and two small children in tow. They headed to England first, then to America. My mom remembered coming across the ocean on their adventure to freedom. They fled after socialism, and after the Nazis destroyed a once-great country. (National socialism in Austria was the precursor of German Nazism—its failures led to the Nazi occupation.)

Austria's downfall began after World War I, when three major political groups vied for power—the Social Democratic Party of Austria, the Christian Social Party, and the nationalist Greater German People's Party. The socialist democrats wanted a union of German and Austria within the German state. They led the government from 1918 to 1920, and during that time, the country became plagued with severe economic problems. There was a loss of industry, hyperinflation, and escalating political tension.

Profiting from the lingering financial crisis, Hitler's party was doubling its membership every year. One of its party slogans was "500,000 unemployed—400,000 Jews—simple way out; vote National Socialist." In 1938, antisemitism against Austrian Jews rose immediately; Aryanization began when thousands of motor vehicles were seized from their Jewish owners.

During the next year, the government seized about 44,000 apartments in Jewish possession. My grandmother's apartment was taken in one of these invasions. While that was happening, Jews, including my grandfather, were forced to put on their best clothes and clean the sidewalks on their hands and knees.

From March to November 1938, 130,000 people managed to escape legally or illegally from Austria, including my mother and grandparents. These were the lucky ones.

My mom's Alzheimer's was advancing. She would talk about the past and mumble nonsensical things. She did this months before that first call where the facility threatened to "throw her out on the street" after I refused to pay their ridiculously inflated billing. They weren't providing her with the care they were billing for—it seemed reasonable to not pay for things that weren't provided. After the threat, I reached out to the ombudsman and begged for help. Little did I know that this would spark a fire that would continue to smolder.

She whispered strange things to my oldest daughter and me about money and the police. She said that there would be a "big court case." It sounded like her Alzheimer's was creating paranoia. Looking back, it wasn't Alzheimer's Disease. She knew what was about to happen, and at the time, I didn't.

When the civil suit was filed by the nursing home, I wasn't initially concerned. It seemed like a monetary dispute that could be resolved. There was a bill for her care and a disagreement about that bill; it seemed like one of those things that could be worked out.

I should have Googled the law firm that was representing the nursing home, but I didn't. I was too wrapped up in other things that I thought mattered more. I should have paid more attention to the news buzzing in South Florida and around the country about guardianships and the elderly. There were so many things I should have done, so many mistakes that I made.

When they wanted a court-appointed guardian, I stupidly embraced the idea. Finally, there was someone to advocate for my family. You know that phrase, "you don't know, what you don't know." That sums it up. For years the guardianship system throughout the country has failed to protect incapacitated seniors. Its purpose has become a distant memory, in many cases and instead, it's morphed into a perverted system. The individuals benefiting are no longer the elderly; instead, they are greedy attorneys and professional guardians.

If I had simply Googled the lawyers representing the case, I would have seen *The Palm Beach Post* headline, "Jury Hits Lawyers with $16.4M for Doing Senior Wrong in Guardianship."

According to that article, attorneys Brian M. O'Connell and Ashley N. Crispin not only breached their fiduciary duty, but also committed professional negligence. If I had read the article, I would have seen Julian Bivins' quote, who brought the suit as the personal representative of the estate of his father, Oliver: "It's really kind of a landmark case. It sends a message to these unscrupulous lawyers and guardians that they are not going to be able to get away with it anymore."

Sadly, that case didn't end anything. This judgment seemed to be just a bump in the road. It was after this judgment, that the law firm came for my mother, and then they came for me. It wasn't a shocker that the law firm was politically connected to Democrat politicians for generations. Brian O'Connell was the nephew of Phillip O'Connell, Sr. who served a quarter-century as the state attorney for Palm Beach County. A bust of him graces the lobby of the State Attorney's office.[1]

These players had their share of national headlines. Roughly ten years ago, one of the named partners in Phillip's law firm, Bill Boose, was sent to prison for fifteen months after admitting he helped former Palm Beach County Commissioner Tony Masilotti hide profits from a secret land deal.[2] The scandal also sent Masilotti to prison and rocked the county.

These were the Democrat players, but I didn't know who I was dealing with. My mother died at the hands of a neglectful nursing home that was cuddling up with a law firm entrenched in the swamp of Florida.

Democrats want to socialize health care but have left the elderly to die. They shifted them around nursing homes in New York City during Covid, sealing their fate.

The history was always there for us to see; we should have heeded the warnings. In a 2011 video with the Daily Caller, Democrat presidential candidate Michael Bloomberg said that elderly cancer patients should be denied treatment to cut health care costs while visiting a grieving family whose brother had died after reportedly waiting seventy-three hours in an emergency room. "All of these costs keep going up, nobody wants to pay

[1]   Sun-Sentinel, "PHILLIP D. O'CONNELL, EX-JUDGE, STATE ATTORNEY," Sun Sentinel, September 22, 1987 https://www.sun-sentinel.com/news/fl-xpm-1987-09-22-8703180182-story.html

[2]   Sun-Sentinel, "Attorney Indited in Land Deal," Sun Sentinel, November 4, 2006 https://www.sun-sentinel.com/news/fl-xpm-2006-11-04-0611040069-story.html

any more money, and at the rate we're going, health care is going to bankrupt us."

Bloomberg, who was then New York City's mayor, went on to say, "We've got to sit here and say which things we're going to do, and which things we're not, nobody wants to do that. You know, if you show up with prostate cancer, [and] you're ninety-five-years-old, we should say, 'Go and enjoy. Have a nice [inaudible]. Live a long life. There's no cure, and we can't do anything'. If you're a young person, we should do something about it. Society is not ready to do that yet."

Socialism is a slippery slope. The Democrat party has been overrun by a socialist agenda. Do you think the families in Austria would have imagined what socialism would do to them?

There are many similarities between what happened then and what is happening now. It came as no surprise to me that there was a tie to the Democrat party in my case. They were just too focused on taking down another Republican Conservative, while ignoring that an elderly woman was left to die. Maybe they would have treated my mom differently if they knew she was a Democrat.

"The man who has no sense of history is like
a man who has no ears or eyes."
—*Adolf Hitler*

Chapter 11 —————————————
Political Segregation

Mr. Daniels was that teacher that everyone wished for, and I had hoped he would be my teacher in fourth grade. He had a warm, friendly smile, and his relaxed attitude was apparent in the way he dressed. His preferred attire was light brown corduroys and plaid button-downs. He knew an endless playlist of songs that he seemed to effortlessly turn out on the piano. If you were the lucky kid that day, you won the honor of sitting beside him as he played, watching his Hush Puppies dance on the foot pedals.

Mr. Daniels introduced our class to Stevie Wonder and Paul McCartney's "Ebony and Ivory," which was the song we opened our concert with and one of the biggest hits of 1982. Mr. Daniels told us that the inspiration for this song came when Paul McCartney heard Spike Milligan say, "Black notes, white notes—you need to play the two to make harmony, folks!" We knew the song was about racial harmony, but we didn't realize that this was something our town had worked hard to achieve during our childhood.

My mom chose Teaneck as our home. My dad had been interested in other cities, but she got to make the final decision. (He said, "It was better for me that way.") She chose Teaneck, not for its walkability and large population of Jewish families but for another reason entirely.

The school gym and auditorium were one and the same. There were tables that folded up against the walls when they weren't being used; when they were unfolded, they revealed benches for lunchtime. At the end of the room, there was a stage, which functioned as the setting for many concerts and plays throughout the year. The windows were flanked by giant blue and green lantern-patterned curtains, hung from the ceiling to the floor, and the stage curtain perfectly matched these oversized curtains. It was an all-purpose room in every sense of the word and was used for everything from lunch to Girl Scout meetings and gym class. During elections, it was even transformed into a polling location. Our neighborhood school was idyllic, and it never occurred to me that racial differences existed until after sixth grade.

I, of course, noticed that the majority of my black friends rode the bus. I walked a short distance to school—from my house, down the winding street of Standish Road, past the family with the bunnies in the yard. In my mind, we were all Lowell kids; there was no difference if you rode the bus or walked to school.

Teaneck's racial divide was brought on by housing practices that forced black families into the northeast section of town. It was a suburb where residents fought blockbusting attempts by planting defiant "Not For Sale" signs on their front lawns. Their attempts were recognized, but there was still a divide, which left the schools in that area separate and unequal. However, the houses were similar in both sections of town, and there were not the economic differences that some communities faced.

In 1964, Teaneck was the first town in the country to have voluntary integration. Superintendent of Schools Dr. Harvey B. Scribner was the heroic captain at the helm, steering Teaneck into these unprecedented waters. That year, the conversion of one of the town's schools created central sixth grade. There were no protests or violence. It all happened quietly for the benefit of the entire community. The school board moved quickly, and the residents embraced it.

My mom chose Teaneck because she wanted inclusiveness for all people. She imagined that there was no color. Even into her later years, she always had a variety of friends in ethnicity and personality. She would often seek out someone who was new to town—many times, they were immigrants that my mom made an effort to include.

This was one of the many reasons she thought she identified with liberal viewpoints. This was a misunderstanding—many of these are merely human viewpoints. She was misled by her own party, like so many.

The Democrat party isn't really inclusive. It's a branding illusion that utilizes a false narrative and the news media to create the divisiveness that she opposed. My mom was a socially inclusive person who gave herself the label of Democrat. She concerned herself with the issues that were of importance to her and shrugged off the other issues that didn't emotionally strike her.

I think too many people do this; this leaves them susceptible to the elitist sector of the party, which doesn't serve the real people. It's filled with old money donors that don't have their real interests at heart. They label themselves inside a party that carries social ideals that they want to embrace and identify with a party that makes promises that make them feel good, but failure lies in the actual execution of commitments. Historically there is little in return for that investment of loyalty, and the elitists always win.

In the 1960s and 1970s, social issues were at the crux of my mother's choice to label herself as a liberal Democrat. There were some things that I could understand about her position on politics—most notably Civil Rights issues and human issues. (Imagine how much better America would be if we focused on things that unite us rather than divide us.)

When my mom was eighteen, she began attending Brooklyn College, which was a short bus ride from where she lived. The headlines of 1954 included the case Brown v. Board of Education, which was acknowledged as one of the most significant Supreme Court decisions of the twentieth century. It unanimously held that the racial segregation of children in public schools violated the Equal Protection Clause of the Fourteenth Amendment. Although the decision did not fully desegregate public education in America, it put the Constitution on the side of racial equality and galvanized the Civil Rights movement into a full revolution.

My mother was a conservative at her core; she didn't teach for more than a year or two before deciding to become a homemaker. She wanted to be home with her child while her husband worked. I am glad she made this decision; my life would have been a lot less colorful if I she wasn't at my side.

When she was at her weakest and most vulnerable, I was in crisis. The alligators started to swim around us. When they attacked with the lawsuit, I wasn't prepared. I didn't grow up in the swamp, and I never learned how to wrestle or trap gators. I was naïve about the guardianship system and the way lawyers profit.

I was also not informed of the historical connections of the law firm the facility was using. Its partner's family roots be traced in the Florida swamp going back to the turn of the last century. The O'Connell clan was rich with political connections in Florida. Ironically, after the headlines broke, the first op-ed appeared in *The Palm Beach Post*; it predicted how I would get off easy because I was politically connected. It also noted that the charge was a misdemeanor and that I would be able to retain my right to vote. This seemed to infuriate the author who wrote, "Thank God it wasn't an unconnected minority who did this. That poor soul would face years in jail." There certainly seemed to be politics at play, and it didn't seem to be my connections that were pulling the strings.

Stephen O'Connell went on to be an iconic figure in University of Florida history as its resident and was an active member of the Democrat party. Good ol' Stephen was also appointed as a justice in the Florida Supreme Court back in 1955. These days his name graces the basketball arena, known as The O'Connell Center. Construction was completed in December 1980, and the first touring event was The Harlem Globetrotters.[3] In the university's handbook for employees of the center it states: "It is fitting that such an outstanding facility be named for such an outstanding individual."

I wonder how the Harlem Globetrotters would have felt back then and how today's college students playing basketball would feel if they researched history. Stephen's time on the Florida Supreme Court followed the U.S. Supreme Court's decision in

---

[3] "Who Is Stephen C. O' Connell?" Stephen C. O'Connell Center (University of Florida), https://www.oconnellcenter.ufl.edu/about-us/history/

striking down "separate but equal" segregation as violating due process in Brown v. Board of Education.

Mr. O'Connell's judicial philosophy was in opposition. He believed—despite the Supreme Court's decision three years earlier—that integration should be further delayed because "violence in university communities and a critical disruption of the university system would occur if Negro students are permitted to enter the white state universities at this time, including the Law School of the University of Florida, of which it is an integral part." After serving in this position and even serving as chief judge briefly, the Florida Board of Regents selected him to be the University of Florida president later in 1967.

When Stephen O'Connell became president at the University of Florida, many of its black students (a small population on campus) were actually foreign exchange students. The Black Student Union organized a sit-in protest in an office suite in 1971 for a black cultural center. The occupation ended with the arrest of the students, which occurred after O'Connell threatened them with expulsion. In the aftermath of the sit-in, O'Connell refused to grant amnesty to the student demonstrators who had participated. Many of the black students and faculty members left in protest.

O'Connell's legacy wasn't about his interactions with students or their well-being on campus during his tenure—it was all about his political connections and donors. The University of Florida website eliminates this history and states, "During his six-year term, 1967-1973, he guided the university through a tumultuous era of student protests. He oversaw the integration of the university and reorganized the alumni association and advancement programs."

As usual, money wins in the end, and the other facts are left out. O'Connell's most significant legacy wasn't the cultural scandal; it involved his ability to change the opinions of state legislators who had previously opposed large-scale, private fund-raising. The ability to have connections that lead to money is the legacy that the university celebrates today.

Immigrants made up the fabric of America. My mom's heart was always in its people—she had friends of every race and color. This never changed. She was an immigrant girl, and everyone was like her.

In August 1963, she boarded a bus for Washington D.C. to stand in the Lincoln Memorial's shadow as 200,000 people gathered in peace to demand equal justice for all citizens. She was there as Martin Luther King, Jr., gave his "I Have a Dream" speech, which emphasized his faith that all men, someday, would be brothers. The rising tide of the Civil Rights Movement and the peaceful Americans who stood steadfastly in support influenced national opinion. In 1964, the Civil Rights Act was passed, guaranteeing equal voting rights and outlawing discrimination. The Civil Rights Act encouraged school desegregation, that was opposed by O'Connell in the Democrat swampland of Florida.

South Florida has filled in most of the swamp, creating its version of suburbia with gated neighborhoods resembling small towns. The swamp is just beneath them, piling up fill on top of what once dominated the landscape, replacing it with canals and retention ponds. The alligators have adapted and found a way to keep breeding. You don't need to look far beyond the surface to realize it's still the same swamp.

"Let people not say that Teaneck waited to be directed. Let them say Teaneck led the way."
—*Harvey Scribner, Superintendent of Teaneck Schools*

Chapter 12 ————————

For Such a Time as This

𝕵n Teaneck, with its manicured lawns, Tudors and Colonials, and integrated schools, there was also a Hebrew school. Teaneck was a testament to minority groups thriving in suburbia, and in 1940, Jews constituted roughly 1 percent of its population. At that point, there was twist of fate—"beshert," as we call it. In Yiddish, it means inevitable or preordained; it can apply to any happening which appears to bear the fingerprints of divine providence.

In 1959, the mayor's death put a Jewish deputy in the town seat. Matthew Feldman took an aggressive stance in his new position. He told *The New York Times* that there was no Great Wall of China surrounding the town, and anyone not satisfied with our suburban melting pot was free to leave.

By 1960, Jews accounted for 20 percent of the town's residents. In the 1970s, it was one-third of the residents and eventually grew to about 4 percent. Teaneck's Jewish and black communities had forged a united front; they stood up against racism to improve the town for its residents.

On our side of town, there were more religious folks, walking through town in a pilgrimage to temple, of which there were many. I always thought this was very reminiscent of the stories I had learned of my Jewish ancestors wandering through the desert.

As a sign of my mom's progressiveness, we belonged to a reform temple—her reasoning was feminism and inclusivity. The influences of contemporary societal norms had changed many of the religion's traditions in reform temples. Men and women could sit together, and women were allowed on the bimah, which was forbidden in other sects. They were also permitted to participate in parts of the service that were traditionally restricted to men.

My father would have preferred a conservative or Orthodox temple, as he was very devout in his love of religion and history. However, my mother, again, won this decision. My dad had one caveat—we never drove to the temple. We walked as the observant Orthodox Jews did. This wasn't so hard for me, as my regular days consisted of walking and bus rides with my mom.

Luckily our little white temple, Temple Beth Am, was a short walk from our house. It had once been a little white church, so the steeple remained, but it was now adorned with a Star of David. It was small and warm and had a great library filled with books that opened the other way. Every week, we were encouraged to take out books after our classes were done.

My favorite books were about Queen Esther, who was the Jewish queen of a Persian king. Her story starts with King Ahasuerus drunk at a festival, who ordered his queen, Vashti, to appear before him and his guests to display her beauty.

She refused to appear, so the drunk king immediately banished her and sought a new wife. He held a beauty contest, and the winner was Esther. She was the biological cousin of Mordecai, a member of the Jewish community. As the orphaned daughter of his uncle, Mordecai wanted her to have a better life, so he raised her and cared for her as her adoptive father. Esther was under strict instructions from Mordecai to conceal her Jewish origins. Her stunning beauty made the king fall in love. She won the contest and became queen.

Later, Mordecai refuses to bow to Haman, who was the king's highest advisor. This set off Haman, who took his ego-driven personal hatred towards Mordecai to another level. Haman convinced the king to order all Jews should be killed. Mordecai tells Esther that she must tell the king she is Jewish and ask him to repeal the mandate to kill her people.

Esther was terrified and knew she could be put to death. She tries to tell him but lacks the courage and instead tells him she needs something from him, but she doesn't reveal what it is. The king assures her that he will give her anything that she wants, but she doesn't trust that he won't turn on her.

Instead of telling directly, she comes up with a strategy. Esther invites the king and Haman for a feast the next day. The king stands up at the dinner table, professes his love for her and publicly asks Esther what it is she wants.

This time she speaks up and says she is being threatened. When the king asks who is responsible, she names Haman. The king orders Haman to be put to death by hanging. Esther then asks him to revoke the declaration to kill the Jews and tells him about Mordecai's role in her life as her adopted father.

The king rewards Mordecai by making him his highest advisor and gives carte blanche to Esther and Mordecai to immediately send out an order in the king's name that gives all Jews the freedom to assemble and defend themselves. They can also kill anyone who threatens them or their families and even seize their riches from the day that Haman's order was supposed to go into effect. The Jews fight back, and in a twist of fate, their enemies are slain.

The holiday of Purim celebrates this fateful day. As a Hebrew school student, it was my favorite holiday. Our little temple didn't have a Purim celebration, but the more prominent congregation across town did. Their massive ballroom was filled with games and activities. There was the goldfish game where participants could win a live goldfish. It was exhilarating! You would tote the goldfish around with you all day in its plastic bag. It would stay alive for that day, but typically not much longer. There were many colorful carnival games with colorful balloons that you could pop with a dart on a board to win prizes and little white monsters with fur-trimmed heads that you would throw balls at to knock off a shelf. It was glorious.

The room was filled with costumed biblical characters of different heights and ages. Most of the girls (like me, of course) arrived decked out as Queen Esther. We wore crowns, long dresses, and strings of Mardi Gras-type beads piled on top of each other around our necks. Most of the boys were King Ahasuerus, but their costumes lacked the historical details that ours had. Some were as simple as a paper crown with their regular clothes. There were also a few Mordecai's peppered in. There was a moment we would all wait for anxiously—the bold, grand finale, which began with loud music. An emcee would take the stage, and the evil Haman entered the ballroom with much fanfare. Wielding plastic blow-up bats, we would beat this wicked, bearded man to a pulp.

The morning started like many others in my house, with Fox News droning in the background. As usual, my husband was getting dressed and looking for accessories for the day's outfit. "Does the pocket square match? Where is my gold Remington tie clip? The one that was your dad's. I want to wear it."

As I put on my makeup, my many distractions were evident. I was juggling plates—I worried about getting my son off to school, my mom's worsening health, and work deadlines. Regardless, I wanted to be on-time, instead of running my usual ten minutes late. Our agenda for the day seemed like a small blessing in light of another chaotic mess.

The sun was out; it was fall but we were still experiencing the heat of summer. It's the usual South Florida blessing and a big attraction in living here, but the beautiful warmth was brief, as we headed into the massive judicial complex's massive looming visibly in front of us. The building's negativity permeated out onto the enormous courthouse steps—it felt like it was at a lower vibration than the streets of West Palm Beach surrounding it.

A windy vortex greeted us as we entered. The toxic energy from arguments and lawsuits lingered in every hallway. Some of the lawyers and judges resembled zombies going through the motions each day; they were the walking dead of traffic or foreclosure court. Then, there were the predatory professionals suing for sport and profit in civil and family courts.

There was another breed altogether—the vultures. These are the ones who pick on the bones of the dead. As I walked in, I remind myself there are good lawyers, who litigate against the wrongdoing of the system. I am married to one.

Why do they want a sole guardian so badly? Why is it wrong to appoint a neutral co-guardian to help the professional guardian? After all, she's an independent professional? Why the opposition to this logical suggestion? The negative thoughts started to creep in as the judge heard the case. The civil lawsuit over the nursing home bill has led to so much contempt between me and the nursing home. *Maybe they could actually do their job and take care of my mom.*

I disconnected my gut feeling about the guardian because she was too much to bear at that moment. As I watched her from across the room, she appeared to be way too friendly with the law firm. My questions mounted, but the judge's ruling meant there was no additional time to question.

I approached Ashley Crispin, Brian O'Connell's legal partner, in the hall. She wore the same black pantsuit, which appeared to be her daily uniform. Her stringy blonde hair appeared unusually unkempt.

She walked away as I approached the new guardian, Amy. This new "advocate" was not warm and friendly, and my negative thoughts were still swirling. I asked her if she will be able to go with me to see my mom that afternoon; she told me she had a scheduling conflict. I asked her if tomorrow might work, and she explained that she couldn't commit, but she will call me, or I can call the law firm.

In Judaism, fallen angels rebelled against God. They were led by sin. Since the dawn of mankind, evil has challenged man and provides an explanation of why pain and suffering come upon those who do not deserve it. When I was naïve, the word "guardian" invoked the emotions of a watcher, a caregiver, an angel. The Guardian Angels of my childhood were the good souls, the guardians in the red berets.

This guardian seemed to be something else.

Haman was a fallen angel who had it all—political power, honor, and wealth. His inflated l ego got the best of him, and he screwed it all up. He allowed one person to get under his skin and ordered the destruction of everyone like him. He needed Mordecai to bow at his feet; he wanted to feel superior.

Esther took part in a beauty contest staged to win the position of queen. She had no powerful connections; she didn't come from the nobility. It wouldn't have entered anyone's mind that her beauty would result in powerful political influence. She was merely the product of a concerned adoptive father.

On the day that the Jews were supposed to be slaughtered, Haman gives himself a gift—a seventy-five-foot gallows built so he could fully savor Mordecai's demise. That was where Haman was hung for everyone to see.

> *"For if you keep silent at this time, relief and deliverance*
> *will rise in another place, but you and your father's*
> *house will perish. And who knows whether you have*
> *not come to the kingdom for such a time as this?"*
> —*The Book of Esther*

Chapter 13 ───────────

Mafia Wars

The streets of New York City were always rough before Rudy Giuliani cleaned up the city. Back then, he was the United States Attorney for the Southern District of New York.

My record collection was growing in 1985. I had gotten my hands on several new albums after some cumbersome allowance negotiations with my mom. My latest additions included Prince and Tom Petty.

Around the World in a Day was Prince's album following *Purple Rain*. On this album, Prince experimented with psychedelia. It was opulent but with an eclectic vibe. "Pop Life" was my favorite song—I played it over and over. The album drew numerous comparisons to The Beatles' *Sgt. Pepper's Lonely Hearts Club Band*. Prince said, "The influence wasn't the Beatles. They were great for what they did, but I don't know how that would hang today. The cover art came about because I thought people were tired of looking at me. 'Who wants another picture of him?' What would be a little more happening than just another picture would be if there were some way I could materialize in people's cribs when they play the record. I don't mind [the album being called psychedelic] because that was the only period in recent history that delivered songs and colors. Led Zeppelin, for example, would make you feel differently on each song."

Tom Petty's latest hit was "Don't Come Around Here No More" from his *Southern Accents* album, which didn't resemble much that was actually Southern. The video for the hit song featured Alice, from *Alice in Wonderland*. The scene opens with Alice amidst giant mushrooms where she encounters a man smoking a hookah while perched on top of the fungi. Tom Petty was the Mad Hatter. The song was a departure from everything else he had done before; he had even mixed in Indian influences. All the drug references on both albums were completely lost on me.

This musical backdrop was happening at the same time that our nightly news was peppered with stories about organized crime. From early 1985 until late 1986, eleven mob figures, including the heads of New York's so-called "Five Families," were indicted with U.S. Attorney Giuliani leading the charge. Giuliani's goal was to wipe out the New York mafia.

Watching the news each night was like an episodic series of *The Godfather*. It looked like Hollywood fiction, but reality spilled out onto the streets of Manhattan. On a December evening, on a crowded street, Paul Castellano had just finished a steak dinner in Midtown Manhattan, as four assassins approached, conspicuously dressed in trench coats and Russian fur hats. He was gunned down in the brazen hit, and John Gotti succeeded as the leader of the Gambino family. The mob under Gotti was like a made-for-TV movie, complete with a dapper, silver-haired leader in expensive suits. Gotti was a media celebrity—he lived large in front of the cameras. When he was on the front page of a newspaper, that edition would sell out. He was a reality star before there were reality stars; he was an old movie mob boss with modern class. Gotti would dine in Little Italy, exiting his black Mercedes with his entourage and the paparazzi in tow. The attitude in New York seemed to be that mobsters killing other mobsters wasn't a problem. After all, they weren't murdering the innocent. These were the same families that controlled our garbage trucks. In Teaneck, they requested a tip, and you needed to show your appreciation during the holidays. If you forgot, you might find garbage strewn across your front lawn.

Gotti seemed like any New York Italian—he was a big personality and the life of the party. He was rumored to hold court at a piano bar and have Jackie "the Nose" D'Amico drop $100 bills on the pianist to play "Wind Beneath My Wings" on repeat. It was hard to see the dark side as you watched him on television; his charm was a great cover for who he really was.

Gotti had Castellano murdered. He didn't like the boss's recent instruction not to trade in drugs. Gotti continued to have his people trade heroin because the profits were too good to pass up. Yesterday's heroin has since been replaced with today's fentanyl.

In 2018, my ex-husband, Nick, was found dead at fifty-seven, while I was dealing with my mother's guardianship. I was fighting with the nursing home, lawyers, and the ligation that tied my hands behind my back.

Nick was found unresponsive in his hotel room. Private investigators and law enforcement couldn't answer the questions, and the last person we believed saw him alive was afraid for herself. He seemed so much to have so much ahead, so many plans. I tore through every shred of information I could grab, and there were just no real answers.

The grief I felt was enormous and matched his colossal personality. My brain was doing cartwheels all day, every day, over the details. *Why was his phone scrubbed clean of all its data? Where was his laptop? Why did he cancel his dinner that night? Why was his family so quick to want to sweep everything under the rug? Was the dancer telling the truth?* These thoughts ran through my head all day and night. None of it added up.

I kept replaying our last conversation, which ended without a goodbye. I told him he was an "asshole" jokingly, and his response was, "but I'm your asshole." In my head, like a song on an endless repeat, I felt a responsibility for my "asshole." I had to fight for him and his memory. My private investigator was thorough, staying in the room next to where he died and pounding the pavement in Charlotte, but had experienced the same dismissive attitude that I had encountered from law enforcement. "This was an overdose," the sergeant said. "Frankly, if we spent a lot of time on each overdose, we'd have big problems."

When asked if they saved the surveillance video, the sergeant said they watched it and saw a female matching the description of the dancer leaving the lobby that night. "We watched it, but didn't ask the hotel for a copy," he said. "Now I wish we did because this thing is like a boomerang."

The dancer claimed two cops interviewed her at headquarters in downtown Charlotte for ninety minutes. "She came downtown to pick up her phone," he said, "but I do not indicate the file that we interviewed her. As far as I'm concerned, she refused to be interviewed." he added. "We didn't have enough to charge her. We have to go with the policy of the DA's office."

The private investigator asked the police to view the file, but they declined. "There's nothing in it anyway," he said. "Like I said, there wasn't a lot of investigating in this case." In a state where the police aren't required to release files as public records, the courts do little to help those trying to get answers. We were hitting a wall.

The hotel installed a few security cameras in the lobby after he died and acknowledged that there was only one camera in the entrance at the time of his death. Its location would not have shown the woman's face.

The manager was the first person on the scene. "I knocked and didn't hear anything, so I yelled 'room check.'" There was no answer. So, I figured the person was asleep, and I told the front desk to give him until three in the afternoon. We didn't need the room that day. I went back at three, and again no answer. This time I told him through the door, he'd have to pay for an extension or another night, and I would be back at three-thirty."

The dancer told the private investigator that she arrived at the hotel around noon when the app showed her that her cellphone was there. The manager said he had no knowledge that a woman came in who'd lost her cellphone. "People lose a lot of things in a hotel," he said. "I've got a guitar case and a fake leg in my lost and found closet right now." He was quick to add, "We found his rental car in a strange place down the street, four days after the body was discovered."

The P.I. received a call from the sergeant the day after they spoke. It matched what the dancer told him. Detectives did interview her, and she told them the same story. "I'm sorry I told you she refused to be interviewed," the sergeant said. "Frankly, with our caseload and the increase in opioid overdoses, cases like this one are starting to all run together."

The sergeant also changed the story from the initial interview and came to the conclusion officers never looked at the surveillance video. "Last year, my squad handled ninety-four suspicious deaths; we didn't do much work on it." He added sergeant that the dancer came back to the police headquarters that very morning. "It was the strangest thing," he said. "She stayed for a few minutes and appeared to want to know if she was on the hotel surveillance video. She said, 'I'm wondering if you guys would call me if you saw me on the video,' I asked her if she was in the room. She got pretty angry and said she wasn't."

The hotel manager said, "It's an image that I'll hold forever. It looked like he sat at the edge of the bed and tried to get up, but he fell back down. His eyes were wide open. I felt his forehead with one finger, and he was cold."

Nick was just gone, wiped off the earth in a split second with a lethal dose of fentanyl in his system. He never ingested a drug, not once in eight years we were together. The system had failed us; no one seemed to care besides me.

Prince was also fifty-seven when he was found unresponsive in an elevator at his studio compound in 2016. His death sparked a national outpouring of grief and prompted a joint investigation by Carver County and federal authorities to find out how and why he had died.

An autopsy found the cause of death to be an overdose of Vicodin laced with fentanyl. There was no way to figure out how he got it or if he even knew what it was. His death is a very public example of the nation's opioid crisis and highlighted the challenges of achieving successful police investigations. His estate was left in shambles, just like so many others.

In 2017, Tom Petty was unconscious at his home, not breathing and in cardiac arrest. He was struggling with hip pain and life on the road and had been mixing prescriptions. He was found with lethal doses of fentanyl in his system.

Yesterday's Italian mafia have been replaced with Mexican drug cartels. They are using our venerable southern border as an access point for moving their goods. Currently, Customs and Border Protection scans less than two percent of privately owned vehicles and sixteen percent of all commercial vehicles. Top government officials consistently raise concerns that they don't know what is coming through the border.

Ninety percent all fentanyl seizures occur at legal points of entry. There is a common misconception that China is to blame. "Just blame the Chinese" is an easy go-to. Although much of this dangerous drug is manufactured in China, the days of it being mailed into our country are behind us.

The real problem lies in the Southwest. In 2018, the White House stated it seized almost 5000 pounds of fentanyl at the border—enough to kill every American four times over.

The war on drugs began with President Nixon fifty years ago, and we have had a piss poor history of winning it. President Trump picked up where we failed miserably. In 2019, he gave nearly $2 billion in new grants to help states fight the opioid crisis and prevent more American lives from being lost. In 2020, when COVID hit the U.S., the opioid crisis was erased entirely from the media's narrative. The headlines were replaced by the pandemic, and the lives lost no longer seemed to matter.

"You will never be told when the next bit of education is coming or where it's coming from or who the teacher will be. That information will only reveal itself after the fact."
—Tom Petty

Chapter 14

Justice Winks at Her Friends

"Do you think that a federal prosecutor will charge me?" I couldn't believe these words were coming out of my mouth.

Charge me with what? For not paying the nursing home while they were neglecting her? My head was spinning, and there was a feeling of impending doom. Those clouds were rolling in again. *How could this be happening? After all, it's my mother. I've been her caregiver. I have never had anything more than a speeding ticket. I had no record what-so-ever. No accusations, nothing.* It seemed surreal as law enforcement poked around asking about me. They even showed up at my husband's office to interrogate him.

Meanwhile, they weren't asking me for my story. I kept trying to wrap my head around it. The whole thing felt weird; it was strange and unsettling. I tried to think positively and reassured myself that this was about the nursing home wanting to line its pockets and hide the abuse. I told myself that it would all work out and logic would prevail. I tricked myself, so that I could go through my day without falling apart. *There's no time to fall apart. I don't do that.* I convince myself that I am in a pattern of negative thinking and make up my mind to forget for the moment that we are sitting on top of a swamp.

Guy Fronstin seemed like a logical choice. He was a top-notch criminal attorney that everyone knew. He had worked on the Epstein case and was a regular media guest. We had worked together before, and I liked his style. He was a smooth talker with silver hair, broad shoulders, and a very soothing tone. His clear-rimmed glasses matched the silver streaks in his hair.

Guy was always calm, cool, and collected. He never seemed to get ruffled, even on high-profile cases. He's won cases from murder to DUI. He represented Michael Dippolito when his wife, Dalia, hired a hitman to knock him off. He's also represented the polo mogul, John Goodman, the NFL player, David Boston, and the family of the "Cash Me Outside" teen, Danielle Bregoli, of *Dr. Phil* fame. He's even represented rock legend Rod Stewart.

Of course, it was appealing that he had worked alongside big-name attorneys, including Alan Dershowitz, Roy Black, and Ken Starr. He's appeared on just about every TV news magazine—*20/20, Dateline, Primetime, Geraldo,* and *America's Most Wanted.* I've also worked with Guy on other high-profile cases, including Cindy Yang's.

There was no question that the wolves would be salivating. "Mrs. Florida, an opinionated blonde Republican charged with a crime" was raw meat to them. *Guy Fronstin being a registered Democrat was a bonus,* I thought. *Someone on the other side of the aisle with a long-standing, stellar reputation in the community.* He was working in these courts every day, knew the lay of the land. *Who can better navigate the swamp?* On the day I hired him, his most famous client was a massive case in the headlines—none other than that of Jeffery Epstein. (At that time, Epstein was still alive.)

Guy was calm and reassuring, but I was in full breakdown mode. A breakdown for me isn't a crumpled-up, crying on the bathroom floor. It typically consists of me being enraged. It's refreshing to have someone who makes you feel like everything isn't a big deal. Guy's attitude is one of routine, and nothing is out of the ordinary. Things happen, and I gather that in his day-to-day world of criminal practice, they probably do. I can imagine him talking to Michael Dippolito after he found out his wife hired a hitman. I can hear him calmly saying something like, "Well, she didn't actually kill you. You are still here. This is a positive."

In my daily struggle to be an eternal optimist, it's nice to have someone around who is level-headed. A panic-stricken lawyer, when shit hits the fan, sounds like a horrible idea.

"You should take a voluntary meeting with her [the prosecutor]," Guy said after we chatted about how my mom was doing.

I didn't feel good about it. My head hurt, and I had a bad gut feeling. I tried to push it down and reiterated, "I think she's been worked over by the nursing home and the law firm."

I knew they were throwing accusations around, but I was pretty sure much of the spaghetti they were trying to throw at the wall wasn't sticking. "I feel like she's dirty, Guy. She's jumped in the sack with them, and I can feel it. I've heard how this law firm operates; it is ruthless." I could sense where the prosecutor's alignment was. "There's so much entwinement happening."

Guy assured me that federal courts were different. This wasn't state court—the federal environment was less tainted.

When I started to open my eyes to how they were playing, I began talking to other families. They weren't hard to find—there were plenty of Facebook groups and organizations. There was a massive, connected community of outraged children of elderly parents and relatives. Many of them were scared, broken, and most were broke. They had been worked over in the legal system until they had no more fight left. Their pockets drained with their dignity. I understood, and my empathy for them was easy.

There were also some crazy conspiracy theorists sprinkled in. It was hard to believe the things they said happened to them. Their experiences seemed fictional. I wasn't going to sound like one of them and rant to Guy about the insane stories that I was hearing. After all, he assured me that "federal" courts operated differently. I did question this. "What about my friend Roger? What about all the other people the feds have fucked with?" I wasn't buying it; I wanted to, but I was starting to sweat. I had watched what the FBI and federal courts were doing over the last several years with their blatant overreaching. There were many conservatives facing charges, some of which seemed to be drummed up. Numerous personalities had been banned from social media, like my friends Laura Loomer and Milo Yiannopoulos. So many people on the right were strung up in the headlines, and it was a list that just seemed to grow every day. The cherry on top was the biased media, anxious to cover their antics, and the hunt went far beyond Roger Stone.

Conservatives being targeted didn't start with President Trump. During the Obama Administration, the IRS confessed that it was targeting conservative groups. The Linchpins of Liberty and forty other conservative groups filed suit against the department for having been targeted in their applications for tax-exempt status. Then there was a second case, and NorCal

Tea Party Patriots and 427 other groups joined in to sue the IRS. They also reached a substantial financial settlement with the government. If conservative groups were unable to mobilize, there would be less of a platform and fewer voters engaged.

Later, the outspoken Dinesh D'Souza pleaded guilty in federal court to one felony charge of using a "straw donor" to make an illegal campaign contribution to a Senate campaign. He was indicted for asking some friends to donate money to the campaign of Wendy Long, a Republican who ran unsuccessfully against Democrat incumbent Senator Kirsten Gillibrand in New York in 2012. D'Souza allegedly promised to reimburse them for their donations and ended up being incarcerated for months. Senator Ted Cruz of Texas told *The Hollywood Reporter*, "It's a remarkably selective prosecution, considering Obama raised millions of dollars under similar circumstances and donors merely faced civil fines while D'Souza is charged with felony violation of federal law."

They couldn't stand to lose an election, and when they lost in 2016, that loss kicked off a giant, costly fishing expedition known as the Mueller investigation, which resulted in a whole lot of nothing. They were intent on fighting against President Trump and anyone like-minded, at any cost. The media distracted the public, while the losers made it more difficult for the president to do his job.

Guy's regularly reassuring tone was not convincing this time. I started to question his logic. Is he not seeing the bigger picture? I said, "These connected Democrats are sneaky. I feel like you don't get this angle here. My gut is telling me politics are at play, Guy."

It didn't seem to be registering, or if it was, he was giving me his poker face. There had to be action, and I had to face it. "I

guess putting eyeballs on the situation is better than being blind."
I said, "Set it up. I'll take the meeting with the prosecutor."

I parked across the street. For once, I was early by thirty minutes, giving myself that traffic buffer for the trek up I-95. I had never been to the federal offices before, but they were everything I imagined. Even on the upper floor of the building, you felt like you were in a basement. Walking through the metal detector felt like time-traveling—everything on the inside looks like it's stuck in some weird time warp. The only thing to give away the year you are actually in is the presidential portrait on the entry wall. There may have been windows, but somehow the outdated office decor and everyone's energy sucked out the light.

Once inside, I looked at the massive conference table. On one end, there were stacks and stacks of documents—those with my name on them made me feel violated. As soon as she entered, I felt the temperature drop. *Shit, she matches the profile,* I thought. *She's like every older woman who has a personal, politically motivated gripe with me.*

My mind turned to her political affiliation and her aesthetic as I sat in the outdated meeting space. Yes, I was fully profiling her at that moment. (I am not one to shut off my brain from the apparent signals.) She was tiny and frail in appearance, and her clothes were baggily draping her boney frame. There was an overall misery you could sense, like life has worn her down in this time warp.

As she started to organize her papers, I wondered how old she was. She appeared to be in her late seventies, but maybe she was younger. Perhaps someone hurt her to get her to this place, where she facilitated ripping families apart. It could have been simpler than that—maybe it was just her workplace. Slaving away in this basement we sat in has aged her. She harshly eyeballed me in the way a judgmental, unhappy older woman does.

Guy fielded her pointed questions in his usual mild-mannered tone. She didn't seem to be interested in the facts and appeared to zone out as we spoke to her. It was clear that she had gotten the majority of her information from the nursing home; she said things that weren't remotely accurate, but it didn't seem to be the time for tit for tat. It was clear she was on a mission, and we sat quietly as she poured through her papers, looking for the "gotcha" moment.

"Is that your signature?" she asked.

"It is," I responded. It was clear that she was going to make a point that wasn't going to be easy to argue.

She said, "You couldn't have spent $17,350 on food and housing if your mother was a resident in a facility providing these services."

The care being provided wouldn't have mattered, nor would it have mattered if I bought my mother groceries, vitamins, diapers, and supplies that were better than the home was providing. She was going to find something in her monstrous stack. She was unsympathetic about my mother, the neglect, and the system that had failed. Her eyes were dark and blank when the topic came up, and I knew that she was protecting them. (She sat on the task force for Elder Abuse in Palm Beach County, which was hard to grasp.) I knew that nothing I said would change her position. Her mind was made up before the meeting and long before she found that paperwork.

I was surprised by the way they came for Roger Stone. Two dozen FBI agents surrounded his home on foot, in the air, and even in boats in his backyard at 6:00 a.m. on a Friday.

Of course, CNN was there too. In its video, an agent is seen pounding on the door and announcing, "FBI! Open the door!" He shouted, "FBI! Warrant!" as Roger Stone, barefoot and wearing nothing but a shirt opened the door to find himself staring down the barrel of two assault weapons and a dozen fully-equipped FBI agents.

Stone had been on top before the arrest. The 2017 Netflix documentary *Get Me Roger Stone* captured his branding brilliance, and his eclectic style finally reached the masses. Roger had a unique edge with a Nixon tattoo and signature martinis. His book, *How to Win at Politics, Business, and Style* with a foreword by Tucker Carlson, gives implementable advice from the political genius. The 140 rules include crucial advice like Rule #11: "To Win You Must Do Everything," Rule #95: "Don't Tell Me The Case Tell Me The Judge," and my personal favorite, Rule #99: "Never Pass Up An Opportunity To Have Sex Or Be On Television." Roger's humor and sarcastic wit were real and direct, not bullshit. I liked him immediately when we met. He was selling books and speaking to large audiences.

At that time, Roger was more famous than ever; he was elevated beyond the people who pay attention to history and the political players. He was on the radar of a whole new audience— it was fantastic to watch and well-deserved.

Strategically and powerfully, the swamp rose up in South Florida, and the mighty gators breeding from here to D.C. went in for Roger. The spectacle of the raid executed so publicly seemed to be happening to further poison the jury pool. They wanted to paint him as dirty in the court of public perception and wanted to achieve this with an instant, media-driven result. They created a slanted opinion through television drama. Then they took away his First Amendment rights. How was this America?

"I'm not above the law. No one is. But we don't want to live in a society where Lady Justice has one eye open and winks at her friends and casts the evil eye at her adversaries. When will it stop?"
—Dinesh D'Souza

Chapter 15 ———————————

Betting on Horses

After meeting with the prosecutor and having no confidence in the system, I began to obsessively start doing yoga. I needed to lose myself in something in a big way. It started with a class a week and was quickly growing into a daily addiction. Not that exercise is a bad thing, but I was trading one obsession for another.

My brain was on overdrive: I was overthinking my mom's death and trying to rationalize the unexplainable loss of my ex-husband. The images in my head were vivid and dark. I had so much anxiety over the looming charges, and the constant feeling that I was being picked apart. At the same time, I struggled to be an attentive mother and wife in the shadow of the death of these two people. I was dropping the spinning plates everywhere; I was usually prepared, but the ten minutes late was becoming twenty. The tension was maddening—my hands were trembling, and my mind unable to focus. My hands were eerily similar to my mother's and watching them shake made me take pause.

My mom had some persistent hand tremors that began when I was in middle school. I remember thinking it reminded me of my grandmother. It didn't seem severe, but it was sometimes enough to make my mom stop whatever she was doing. Her headaches were also increasing, and her anxiety was getting worse. Leaving the house meant the stove would need to be checked repeatedly, along with the new addition in our home, an electric dryer, which would need to be unplugged for fear of fire. In our new house, we had a wood stove in the den, a comfortable garage conversion. That fire hazard could certainly never be used—my mother sealed it with masking tape to prevent a mishap.

My father had taken a job in the western part of New Jersey; it was about an hour and a half away from the comforts of home. There was danger everywhere, from the spontaneous combustion of household items to the robbers that might lurk in the undeveloped spaces of our new town.

Hackettstown was the boondocks—you would have thought we moved to the plains of Kansas. We landed in the boonies, practically in Pennsylvania. We were closer to the Appalachian Trail that my mother once hiked in her twenties and further from Manhattan.

We were living on an actual ranch, as far as my mother was concerned. My parents settled on a three-bedroom, ranch-style home on three-quarters of an acre. Our development stood alone amid undeveloped fields behind the M&M plant that surrounded our neighborhood. It reminded me of places we went on vacation in Maine or upstate New York.

Gone was the prevalence of public transportation—trips to the city would be more complicated. The town demographic was also different. Gone were the Friday evening walks to the temple and the security of knowing everyone at school. I would walk to school as I had in Teaneck, but now I would walk past Hackettstown's Main Street, with its quaint shops and stores. It was a pleasant half a mile from where I lived. The next closest town wasn't something you could pop over to on a bus. We were in rural, suburban isolation.

My mom wasn't as active as she had been before. We no longer ran the streets together anymore. There were no subways to explore, no Central Park, and not much of anything. She would walk to town, but something was shifting with her.

I didn't understand it, but I was content to be grown up. It was an adventure to explore as much as I could of our new town on my own. I would ride my black Schwinn 10-speed bike everywhere. I had a new school and cheerleading practice; there were new friends and exciting activities, like tubing in the local river and riding ATVs.

There was only one thing missing that I desperately wanted out of country living—horses. I was drawn to them, and I felt like I belonged on a farm somehow. I had ridden a horse in Central Park once and had been on a pony ride or two. I begged for riding lessons as soon as we moved in, but nothing worked. My mom didn't drive, and my dad was working. My afterschool options were limited, but I was determined to figure it out.

I had remembered seeing them just as we pulled into town, and I rolled down the window to see them better. They were just two miles away, outside of where the highway met the main road. As you descended the hill from the highway, there was a huge barn and beautiful thoroughbreds. I was enamored as they grazed on the huge field in front of the barn. I imagined that, with my small stature at eighty pounds, I might even qualify to be a jockey. I had a feeling they were racehorses, and I knew I belonged with them. After school, I hatched a plan to go there and ask for lessons. Perhaps they would make an exception for a young enthusiast who wanted to ride.

The property was huge, stretching on for what seemed like miles. The dirt road leading to it was rough, so I got off and walked my bike towards the barn and the field of thoroughbreds that I had noticed from the street. There was a farmhouse and several smaller stables. I felt immediately at home. Maybe I lived on a farm in a past life like Laura from *Little House on the Prairie*. It just felt so familiar for a city kid that had only experienced the horses of the urban sprawl in Central Park.

I walked into the barn and was met by the strange stares of several men sitting around a card table yelling at each other. It made me slow my pace for a minute as I walked in. I wasn't sure if they were arguing—I immediately wondered if it was a bad time to make my move.

One of the older men in the group, assuming I was lost, told me to go to the house to use the phone inside. I explained that I was looking for riding lessons. There was silence, then the short, balding man in the group smirked at me and said that this was a barn for racehorses.

"These are horses that go to the track," he said in a gruff voice.

"I knew that," I replied with conviction. This lightened the moment, and they all laughed. I explained that I had watched racehorses on TV in the OTB (Off Track Betting) at the bus station in New York City when we couldn't catch the bus on-time. I also told them that my mom had once purchased a ticket for a horse race on Monmouth Park track, and she won.

They seemed entertained by my story. One of them got up from the table and said that I had a gift for comedy and asked if my mom knew where I was. He took me through the stables and introduced me to his grandson, who was leading an enormous horse into the other side of the property.

The horse and the grandson dwarfed me. He was an older, tall teenage boy, who looked at me as if I had two heads. His grandfather explained that I loved horses and asked him to take me out to see Diamond Jim.

Diamond Jim looked like a doppelgänger of the Marlboro man. He was in cowboy boots, a hat, and jeans. He wore a flannel shirt and had a cigarette perched on his lip. When he smoked, he didn't need hands. The cigarette just dangled from his mouth, even as he talked. "Did you come here on your bike? Did you come from school? Seems like a far ride to get here."

His questioning my ability to travel was a sensitive spot for me. I felt a little judged and explained that my mom didn't drive. He asked me if she was ill, probably assuming there must be something wrong with someone who didn't drive, and I said yes—it was easier than trying to explain her nervousness. In the same moment, I realized anxiety could be debilitating, like an illness.

"So, you want to ride?" he asked.

I responded boisterously, "Yes."

That answer was met with a response that I wasn't prepared for: "This probably isn't the place for that, but if you like horses, it's the place you should be."

I felt like I was being challenged. *Was he questioning my selfish desire to ride horses? Was this selfish? Should I be in this for the dedication to the animals or the love of the sport of horseracing?*

I wasn't sure, and it was unclear to me how to respond. He was a little rough, a little mean, but this made impressing him a challenge, and I wanted to win my new friend, the

Marlboro Man, over. "Yes, I love horses. I might even want to be a jockey someday."

Now he was laughing—this was a good sign. He told me that in a year, I would be too tall, and racetrack jockeys were men, and the sport was dangerous. He went on to give me every reason why I would never be an asset to a racetrack.

The tall teenager was standing by, taking this all in as the Marlboro Man ended his negative tirade by telling me that I would be a liability at a racetrack and would also be in the way at his barn.

I was even more determined now and persisted with my case and my love for animals and the sport. He finally—very reluctantly—offered me a job. I would clean stalls after school for $12 a day. It would teach me about horses, and he might consider letting me ride one of them at some point. There were no promises and guarantees, but I was sold on the possibility.

The next year was challenging for my mom—she was not herself. The move to the country was debilitating for her. She felt trapped by the little town and crippled by anxiety. My father and I saw it. The doctors just saw an unfulfilled housewife and looked the other way at her symptoms. Her hands were trembling from nervousness.

In the present, my nerves were getting the best of me, and I threw myself into a routine. Predictability was comforting in a time of turmoil, like the predictability of my job at the racetrack barn. The horses had predictable expectations. They knew when I would be there, when they would eat, and what pasture we would move them to while we cleaned. It was a job I got lost in, so much so that I almost didn't care about riding.

That was when the Marlboro Man asked me if I wanted to ride the next day. He had one of his personal horses saddled up—western, of course. He gave me a quick how-to and said I was a natural. I felt like I had been riding horses my whole life. His horse Trigger was stable, smart, and well-trained. It was something so different than the interests of my parents. It was different, and I knew that I was different.

"You try to do the best with what you've got and ignore everything else. That's why horses get blinders in horse racing: You look at the horse next to you, and you lose a step."
—Jimmy Iovine

Chapter 16 ————————

Clown Car

Clearing my head was working for me. Media work was on the upswing, with no shortage of news hits throughout the week. I was juggling several high-profile South Florida personalities with problems—A CEO full of plate-lickers looking to take advantage of his generosity and spinning ridiculous press allegations and baseless litigation, a professional athlete with a nasty divorce, lousy attitude, and bad habits, and genius inventor with a disgruntled ex-business partner who he had been banging. All of these distractions made my situation seem less dramatic and surrounding myself with other people's problems was working for me.

Participating in crisis management for clients lets me know who they are; I get to know them on a pretty deep level in handling their media, understanding their problems, and helping them navigate. It's fulfilling, and they are always grateful. As they open up to me, we become a team.

Many of my crisis clients have become our friends over the years. It's bonding when you go through trauma with someone. I don't do drama—I eliminate it and teach them the strategy of managing it without emotion. I can do that for a client because it's not my crisis. It's not the same when it is *your* headline or emergency, however.

Television hosting has always been my favorite side gig, and I also knew I wanted to delve in with my celebrity interviews. I wanted to get behind the press stories and find out who people were. My new show, *Behind the Headlines*, was in pre-production mode, and we had an excellent concept for distribution. I envisioned uncovering what the audience didn't already creating an on-camera relationship with them and the person I was interviewing. Everyone has a public and private persona—I wanted to show the latter.

I was always a fan of Barbara Walters. I heard her, "Wait for those unguarded moments. Relax the mood and, like the child dropping off to sleep, the subject often reveals his truest self." That was my dream.

My celebrity wish list was coming together, and it solid. We had lined up Huey Lewis, a true friend and a favorite to interview; fellow conservative and former soap opera sex symbol Antonio Sabàto, Jr.; Kelsey Grammar, aka, Dr. Frasier Crane, America's favorite therapist; and America's favorite boyfriend, Chris Noth from *Sex and the City*. It was all coming together, but it was falling apart at the same time.

There it was, in black and white on the charging document—a misdemeanor charge for Social Security fraud. It turned my stomach. I knew that I had made many friends in the media and had been a hard ass for my clients. I knew that the charges wouldn't go unnoticed, especially for a former Mrs. Florida. I knew it would be a salacious headline.

I started to think about the haters—the Democrat-tied law firm and nursing home. They were likely celebrating and knew what my fate would be as they cuddled up with the prosecutor. Others ran through my mind at lightning speed, including my first husband, who loved Bernie Sanders. His twenty-year unwavering obsession with me was also still in full force. *He'll certainly rehash all the same stories that he's been telling for two decades, revised to make himself more attractive.* My first husband was certain to surface with an embellished version of a real story that only contains a speckle of truth.

Then there were the internet stalkers and trolls who hide behind their keyboards. I thought of the blogger who dedicated a website to the "ugly truth" about me. I then thought about the low-life basement dwellers who dislike my politics and have un-managed rage—one even looked remarkably like Carole Baskin from *Tiger King*.

Of course, there were my fake friends—the Boca Raton locals. They posted obsessively on Facebook and showed up at every charity event just to be seen. Meanwhile, those same characters walk around town talking shit about everyone else. They keep their social status up by putting on a charade about empowering other women and wear the costumes of wanna-be do-gooders.

Then there are other outliers, like my husband's children's mother, a disgruntled ex who never got over the split after a short-term relationship. There were also employees that I've had to let go over the years, and lastly, estranged ex-family members with entitlement complexes. We all have some of these people in our lives—I live big, so I have a big group. For those folks, I imagined the headlines would add to their self-pleasure. It was finally time for them to get off.

I knew I had to keep the momentum going—what do you do in a crisis? I told myself that I thrived with problems. I repeated a mantra to myself: *You will become your client. It's easy—you will play the role of manager for yourself. You do this for others, and you can do it for yourself.*

The pep talk was hardly working, and I could feel my self-doubt creeping in. I wanted to rewind time; I wanted to go backward and start over.

The phone was buzzing incessantly in my hand, and I placed it on silent. My foreign client looked nervous in front of the camera, and his leg was shaking. I pulled out my favorite trick and distracted him with questions. (This straightforward tactic works.) Our conversation filled the nothingness in the air of the room. I babbled as the television crew shuffled around, setting up the last of the lighting and doing a soundcheck. "Can I get you water? Would you like to get lunch after? How's the puppy doing?" The interviewer is a real pro. One of those journalists who I know is going to probe, but he's prepared. He knows what to do, even if he doubts himself for a minute. *I know what to do,* I reassure myself. *Stay confident.*

I needed to keep going, keep moving. I needed to get to New York City and fulfill my obligations there. My television interview was on the books for weeks with a celebrity-owned network. There was also a film festival out in the Hamptons with Kelsey Grammar, Chris Noth, and the others. *Now is not the time to crash. That's what they want. They want me to be a train wreck, to crash and burn. Please don't give them that. That's what they want.*

On the day of the hearing, I was unperturbed—the newspapers were accurate about that. I knew what was happening. I had a lot of time to process it. Yoga, staying calm, and moving forward were my only options.

I saw her sitting in the back. *Oh great, that Post reporter. Excellent.*

I then saw other reporters and people who didn't belong there. *Why would they be here? Is this entertainment for them?* It was like a clown car opened up, and all the clowns were sitting in the back of the courtroom. *Don't let them distract you, don't let them see you sweat.*

"Do you understand the charge against you is a single charge of Social Security fraud?

"Yes, your honor."

"Do you know that this charge can carry a $100,000 fine and a year in prison?"

"Yes, I do."

I wasn't afraid of those words because the prosecutor had offered a plea deal. I was prepared to pay full restitution and had money that was in question. I had failed to appropriately pass it along to the nursing home, which I was suing for an unlawful death.

I acknowledged that I fucked up. It was my mother's money, after all, and if the government said it needed to be allocated to the nursing home, then I would lose the argument.

I thought taking the plea was the right decision, but I was wrong. I had to deal with the charge on my record and a term of probation. I would undoubtedly make more responsible choices in the future. The judge pointed out that the charge was a misdemeanor and that I would not lose my right to vote. I immediately responded saying that voting was important to me because it was.

As we left the courtroom, the reporters were waiting. They were polite and direct, but we weren't answering questions. We just left it at "additional details will surface to explain my actions."

I called my husband from the car. "Get ready," I said. "The haters are going to have a field day. I'm glad you didn't come with me." I see no reason to subject him to public scrutiny, but it doesn't mean he always gets left out of it.

And there it was, in black and white, the sexy, slanted headline: "Conservative Commentator Karyn Turk Admits to Stealing Mom's Social Security."

It was hard to read—the inaccuracies and bullshit that I was trying to get on the *Real Housewives*. It was a lot to take in.

I kept telling myself to separate my emotions. I kept saying, *You are the client; remember, you are not you.*

I wanted to rewrite the whole thing and take out all the fake news. There were bits and pieces of truth, but the article was like the past stories retold and embellished so often that only speckles of fact remain. "The criminal charges stemmed from an ugly fight in probate court that began when she didn't pay for her mother's expenses at the American Finnish Nursing Home in Lake Worth, records show." Well, that's accurate, at least.

I kept going back to the $16.4 million judgment that the jury awarded the opposition's law firm and knew I needed to hire the civil lawyer that won that case, Ron Denman.

Denman understood the players. He had been on the field with them before. He was one of the good ones and also had a hard time understanding how this could happen. When we discussed his first encounter with Brian O'Connell, it made him sound just like the good-ol'-boy that I perceived. "There's plenty to go around for everyone in the probate court," or something like that was their convo as he walked beside the younger lawyer.

He was giving Denman some advice on how the system worked in these parts. Ron's story reminded me of *The Dukes of Hazard*, and O'Connell struck me as Boss Hogg, who was the dirty commissioner who always seemed to be after the Duke.

Burt Reynolds played Boss Hogg in the movie remake of the classic show. He had been a great South Florida neighbor and was nothing like the character he played. I worked with him for a television series and interviewed him on red carpets. He was on my dream list to interview again and someone who added so much to the swamp. He ran an acting school and mentored young actors; he was a person who would take a young talent under his wing and instill good values in that person.

On occasion, there is decency in the swamp; it's just murky and hard to navigate sometimes, but I knew I had someone in my boat rowing with me. Ron Denman came in and immediately took an oar without hesitation. He promised we would depose the guardian, Brian O'Connell, his partner Ashley Crispin, and the nursing home director, Dan. "We can depose them all. Let's find out what they did and what they know," he said.

"The sports page records people's accomplishments. The front page usually records nothing but man's failures."
—Barbara Walters

Chapter 17 ———————

Baby Bird

That looming courthouse was becoming an all too regular haunt. The civil hearings were full of motions and expensive papers; there were no discussions, as prosecutors pushed the court to make their case. There was no consideration for the death of my mother.

The tunnel in the middle was extra windy as I was looking around for Ron Denman. I was hoping he'd arrive before I had to see any of them, but once inside, I spotted the black pantsuit with stringy blonde hair. O' Connell was also shuffling into the room as he entered, dragging a banker's box on a wheeled cart full of papers.

"Banker's box" is an appropriate name for that item; the amount they have billed for that box is likely more than I have in the bank today. *Motherfuckers—that's literally what they are,* I thought. I realized that this word had a definition that I could use as an applicable term to this hearing.

I looked over at Ron. He appeared ready and confident. He carried only a briefcase and a legal pad. *He travels light, and he's good-looking*, I thought.

His tie was in a perfect Kelvin knot. I noted at his salt and pepper hair, little five o'clock shadow, and his height. I looked down at his left hand, and there was no ring. *Why is this guy single? He's athletic, early fifties, and Jewish—a total catch. There must be something. He's probably picky; he has a specific type. I'll troll his Facebook later and see if I can figure it out.* I scanned my friend database in my head, secretly wondering if I knew someone I could set him up with. (My matchmaking skills have been excellent. In the Jewish faith, three successful *sidduchs* get you to the highest level of Heaven. Allowing for divorce rate these days, it's probably best to add another and stack the deck.)

When the judge came in, we stood. I wondered how many times she's dealt with the dark side. *How can she not see what seems to be so transparent?* I looked behind me to the gallery and saw that the usual reporter is in attendance in a bright, royal blue shirt. *She looks nice today*, I thought. I smiled a half-smile at her and got a half-smile back. *Maybe she will be kind today, but I doubt it. At least her articles draw some attention. She is generating eyeballs for the day when I get up off the floor, and someday, I will fight back.*

Almost immediately, my blood began to boil. The stringy haired attorney took the floor with dramatic delivery. She kept repeating, over and over, "her adoptive mother." It hurt my heart.

I always knew. I think I can remember when it happened—I was only three or four at the time. My mom said she was going to wait until I could grasp the concept. She had to tell me, though—the kids on our block had let the cat out of the bag.

Our street of Grace Terrace in Teaneck was filled with kids. Every house had a few, mine only one. There were also a few older people without kids. Mr. Mayor lived next door and had perfect grass—if our kickball ended up there, it was a problem. There was also Mrs. Weber, who had one the first houses built on the block. She had the most incredible stories and made everyone who heard them feel as if they were in the middle of her remarkable history.

The kids on our block were an active ground and played outside from dawn till dusk. It was a mix of teens and their younger siblings. At that time, I was one of the smallest in the entourage.

I was best friends with Ellen who had older sisters with perfectly feathered hair. They had the dream yard on our street; their father built a playhouse to match their brown Tudor. Their yard also had a sandbox with a vast, towering slide, which seemed almost as tall as the house and had a swing set.

I remember sitting in their sandbox when they started to sing, "You're adopted, you're adopted." I wasn't sure what it meant. My next door neighbor, Eric, a bully about a year older than me, started the song.

I'm not sure if I went home right away or hours later, but as I did, I avoided the cracks in the pavement on my way. *Step on the crack, you break your mother's back*, I thought. I couldn't risk that.

As I ran up the steps to the porch, the aluminum screen door slammed behind me. I continued past the threshold across the enclosed porch, opened the heavy wood front door with the large iron handle and ran upstairs. My mom was there, folding laundry on the bed; it was fresh off the clothesline that cascaded through our backyard.

My parents had two twin beds that sat next to each other. My mother's bed was stacked with fresh laundry, and I popped myself onto the end of my dad's bed. I looked at their matching, green-corded bedspreads and the white laundry, which was as bright as the plastic basket it was in.

I knew I was adopted; I just didn't know what that meant. It didn't warrant a complicated answer, but my mother gave me one.

"Well, you know, Carol, our neighbor, who is pregnant." I did and was intrigued by her basketball-sized stomach.

"Well, I was never pregnant with you. You see, most parents don't get to pick their babies, but you were here first, so I didn't need to get pregnant. We got to take you home from the hospital," she explained. "We were lucky because we got to choose you."

This answer was perfect and all I needed! It made sense. I was just there first, and they picked me. What luck!

My mom probably should have stopped there.

"You know how we read *Are You My Mother?*"

Of course, I did! It was a favorite bedtime book. A mother bird sitting in her nest knows her egg is about to hatch. She leaves to get her baby's first meal and Murphy's law rears its head; while she's gone, the egg hatches. The bird is confused, alone, disoriented, and needed a mother. So, he begins an adventurous search for one. The minutes-old hatchling can't fly, so he hops off on foot.

First, he asks a kitten who can't talk, "Are you my mother?" Then, he asks a hen and dog the same question—they both tell him that they are not related. He next finds a cow, repeats the question, and still turns up nothing. He even calls out inanimate objects. Lost and exhausted, he climbs up on a giant crane. Afraid, he cries for his mother. The crane drops him back into his nest, just as his mother arrives with his food. "I know who you are. You are not a kitten. You are not a hen. You are not a dog.

You are not a cow. You are not a plane, a boat, nor a Snort (pig). You are a bird. And you are my mother."

You know that saying "quit while you're ahead?" The book comparison was a perfect example of that. My mother gave me an elaborate explanation, and my therapy began. I was the random mitten, placed among the food items on *Sesame Street*—it was clear that I was out of place. My identity crisis quietly began.

I spent a lot of time looking in the full-length mirror that hung on the inside of the door of my father's closet in the master bedroom. I realized I looked different. I had blue eyes, blonde hair, and a petite frame. I felt like a little alien being. *Was I Jewish like them? Who was my mother? How did this all work?* I knew one thing, these were my parents, and this identity crisis didn't change my feelings toward them. I love my parents and they were my parents, regardless of how I got to them.

Is this sloppy, insensitive, stringy-haired bitch going to keep saying "her adoptive mother?" She was determined to dismiss our relationship, and I found her tactics nauseating. She was my mother. I was six-days-old when they picked me up from the hospital. My face was getting hot.

She didn't even pronounce her name correctly. If she knew her, she'd be able to do that. The guardian couldn't pronounce it either, even with the regular reminders. *ILL-SA*, I screamed in my head. Not "Elsie" or "Isle" or the other pronunciations they were throwing around.

It was a lot to handle, and I had a hard time shutting up. I grabbed a legal pad and Ron's pen and began to scribble notes to him. "WTF. Can she at least get her name right?"

He glanced and reassuringly patted the pad as if it say, "It's okay, let it go."

Stringy hair exited the center ring, as Ron began his opening. He inserted logic to discredit the dramatic rant and made a passionate stand without drama.

She smirked as she called me to the stand. I knew I was getting under her skin as I pleaded the fifth at her pointed questions. Ron continued objecting, as she rephrased here questions, in an attempt to get an emotional rise from me. *That's not happing today, sweetheart. I'm not letting you get me.*

She asked, "Did you speak to my ex-husband? Did you tell him I was a good actress?" I felt a pang of happiness when I realized she is getting personal. *Oh, this is good. I know just where she's going.*

I responded, "I don't recall saying that. I do recall him referring to you as a rock star." *Is she really going to go there?*

She called her first witness, her ex-husband. I was stunned and laughed on the inside, as he took the stand. Ron looked over at me, and I shrugged my shoulders. I grabbed the pad and scribbled, "Oh, this is great, lol." Ron looked perplexed. I hadn't mentioned it because it didn't seem relevant, and I also didn't think she'd call him in. Her ex began to play his part of the sideshow.

Perfect, this is perfect. I grabbed my phone and pulled up the message as he recited his lines. I was glad I screenshot them, knowing that he would erase them. *Good move, girl!*

I motioned to Ron. "Check these out," and slid the phone across the mahogany table.

For once, I was excited. *What a stupid move*, I thought.

She asked, "Did you know Karyn when she contacted you about your services?"

"No, I didn't," he said. "I told her that you were my ex-wife, and it wasn't appropriate to talk to her. I felt uncomfortable that she contacted me."

Seriously, is this guy for real? He's my Facebook friend and fan. He's a follower who regularly likes my photos and posts. I bit my tongue, not out of anger but to stifle a laugh.

I glanced back at the blue-shirted reporter. *There's that half-smile again, which probably means nothing. Finally, a little gratification in this shit show. This development is fantastic.*

Stringy hair finished her questioning with almost a bow. She surely felt accomplished and delighted to put him on the stand.

Ron stood up, holding my iPhone in his hand. He scrolled and paused one last time, as I saw her ex start to get a clue. He got that "oh shit, my ex-wife is going to kick my ass" look.

"You don't know her? Do you mind if I read some messages?" Ron said. "'Hey, saw you on television, with my friend, so funny, just wanted to say hello, keep on rockin'.'"

Then another: "'Hi Karyn, call me when you get a minute. Here's my phone number.'"

And more: "'Happy B-day!'"

"Can I see those?" she motioned to Ron for the phone as she stood up. He handed the phone to her, and she scrolled. Her next statement was, "No further questions."

The first sideshow act wrapped up, but they brought in another witness, and the theatrics continued for almost three hours. By the time Ron and I exited the courtroom, I felt like the building was a little less looming.

I waited for the blue-shirted reporter's article to hit. *What will the headline be? How will she spin this one? She wouldn't sit there for three hours, diligently scribbling away and not write one.*

The article never came—perhaps what she heard didn't fit the script.

"Yes, I know who you are. You are not a kitten. You are not a hen. You are not a dog. You are not a cow. You are not a boat or a plane or a snort. You are a bird, and you are my mother."
—*P.D. Eastman,* Are You My Mother?

Chapter 18 ———————

Trust Your Gut

"You really can't take any interviews until after your sentencing," Guy said.

I was desperate to tell the story—my mother's story. I wanted to write, to blog, to scream from the rooftops, but I was told to be silent. It was unbelievably hard to bear.

Guy had hired a new associate, David Tarras, a young attorney who had been a public defender. I liked him right away—he seemed tenacious and had jumped into the cesspool of crazy that I was trying to swim out of with both feet.

He was also helping me with some other issues, including a weird stalking situation. A woman who had an uncanny resemblance to Carole Baskin from *Tiger King* who had become completely obsessed with me. (These are typical things that Republican commentators encounter.)

David's addition to my case was positive. I felt like he got it, understanding the political angle and the oddities that made the whole scene a little hard to believe. He was a different personality than Guy, which was refreshing. He had an edge that was going to be helpful. However, he deferred to Guy about addressing my case and the real story until after my sentencing. I knew they thought this was the right thing to do, but I wanted to defend myself, and my gut was pulling at me to go forward.

I had run through the sentencing day in my mind for weeks, eagerly anticipating moving forward and putting this nonsense behind me. I would be waving goodbye to the crotchety prosecutor as I exited the courtroom with my misdemeanor charge and a term of probation. I have always been one to follow the rules before now, so I was ready for this.

The plea deal was agreed to in detail. It was not ideal but certainly better than going to a trial against the feds. I couldn't financially drain our family with a fight that could also take a lengthy emotional toll. It was better to have it over with and move on, and I knew this was on terms that I might not win.

There were also hundreds of thousands in legal fees that I didn't have to invest. I would be spending to save myself from probation, and I was paying back the money in question. To do otherwise would be unfair to my husband and children.

The plea was agreed to by the prosecutor, and my lawyers were satisfied. It seemed reasonable. People make deals all the time—it's less of a drain on them and the system. I paid the restitution, giving back every penny in question and more. It was less than the hundreds of thousands to fight a not guilty plea.

It's okay, I told myself. *I can now focus on what matters.* There was real justice that needed to be served; I needed to continue the lawsuit against the facility. I wanted to hold them accountable for neglecting my mom. *Focus on that fight, the one you can win.* After all, Guy had said, "Prosecutors don't go back on plea agreements. If they did, the whole system would fall apart." I didn't buy it, but there wasn't a better choice. I pushed down the negative thoughts again and attempted to be optimistic.

I knew I had to call her and explain what was happening. When I did, there wouldn't be any judgment. She got my politics, my parents, and she got me.

Her bright Southern accent delivered that distinctive "Hello." My birthmother, Pam, always answered on the last ring before it hit voicemail. Usually, she ran around her stables, tending to her horses with a gun on her hip. She lived on a farm with critters and a koi pond she dug herself on a whim.

Pam lived in New Jersey. She worked at the Monmouth Racetrack, caring for the thoroughbreds. She also served in the Air Force with a distinct love of America and freedom. She was one of those special people who love to fill their brains with useful facts. Her knowledge of topics from trees to dog breeds has always been unmatched. She takes no shit and has always had a stand up attitude.

In 1992, I pushed the blue stroller through the concourse of the airport. The baby slept on the plane on our way to Florida. It was odd to think that I was in the place where I was born, but where I had never really been.

Before my maternal grandmother's Alzheimer's disease took her mind, she told me she was in Florida when the setup happened. It was on one of her many trips to Miami. She visited her brother Bobby's house, when fate struck. *Bashert* again.

There was never a question of why I was adopted. Pam was fifteen when she had me. Even at a young age, I understood that she was in high school at the time, and it would have been impossible for her to raise me. When I turned eighteen, my mom was the first person to excitedly say, "Good, now you can find her."

My mother wanted to know what became of the teen they had learned about in the Florida attorney's letters. He was a mutual friend of both families. It was a story with a beautiful beginning but no chapters after those first few months. I was curious about her but a little apprehensive; you never know if those additional chapters might have been left out of the book for a reason.

I waited a few years before tracking her down. I had already given birth to my oldest daughter. My mother was probing me regularly about the search. In those days, there was no internet; it was before DNA and connectivity. There were phone calls, old phone books, and clues.

Finally, a private investigator tracked her down. She was remarried, and I wasn't sure if it was a good idea for me to pick up and call. I called an adopted friend and asked him to make the call, and he obliged. He called me back to tell me he was 100 percent sure it was her when her response to the date of my birthday was, "Holy Shit!"

Pam had initially grown up in Miami. When the big city became too much for her mom and dad, they thought a move to the country was the best for their pre-teen daughter. They settled in Lake Helen, Florida, but made regular visits back home and kept in touch with their old neighbors.

One of those neighbors was my Uncle Bobby. It was an early spring day in Florida, just before the snowbirds head back north, and my grandmother had made her usual escape to Miami Beach for the winter. She was hiding out the Fontainebleau to escape the Brooklyn winter.

There were several people at Bobby's that day for lunch—neighbors, colleagues, friends, and relatives, including my grandmother's sister, Rosl, who was her dedicated travel partner, and Bobby's daughter, Rita.

The Miami sun penetrated the screened lanai with the crank chalice windows. My grandmother sat next to a stunning young woman in her twenties who held a generously poured glass of Chablis. Her name was Glenna, and she had recently married a colleague of Bobby's.

The men stayed inside making business deals, as the women enjoyed the conversation outside. My grandmother, my relatives, and the new wives of Bobby's business friends all got to know each other. The young woman was very talkative and opened up to my grandmother right away about her latest family drama. She had just discovered her fifteen-year-old cousin, who was formerly Bobby's neighbor, was pregnant.

My grandmother immediately knew this chance meeting was meant to be. "What are the odds? What will they do with the baby?" she asked.

Glenna explained that she had just heard the news earlier that day and wasn't sure, but that adoption was likely the route. My parents had tried to have a baby for six years and had not been blessed. My dynamic grandmother was an action taker, and there was no time to waste. Before the social hour ended, she had an attorney lined up, and her baby plan was in motion.

Walking to the end of the concourse pushing the stroller, I saw Pam immediately; it was a real "holy shit" moment. She was blonde with blue eyes and petite. She was someone who looked like me. My first thought was, *She's amazing, and I can't wait for my parents to meet her.*

I knew a week before the sentencing how things were going to roll. I felt it in my gut again.

As I sat in Guy's office, I noticed the atmosphere had shifted a bit. He had his poker face on. "Guy, I'm not stupid, what's changed?"

He assured me that it was nothing but wanted me to be prepared regarding the plea agreement. Even though the prosecution recommended probation, the judge could always recommend a harsher sentence. "Why would that happen, Guy?" My record is unblemished. I have dedicated myself to charity, and there are dozens of character letters.

The PSI, an analysis from by the U.S. Probation Office, gave me high marks. "I read the PSI. It was awesome. What are you saying?"

"I just want you to be prepared," he said.

"Prepared for what?" *What the actual fuck?* was my next thought. *What about the deal that they don't go back on?* He looked at me from across his desk and leaned back casually in his chair. "Just be prepared."

"Guy, what the fuck!"

"Weeeellllll...." his soothing, soft tone was not working for me. "There are those newspaper articles and the other stuff in the press that might not be looked at favorably."

"Huh?" I reiterated that I haven't talked to the press. I was ignoring every phone call that I desperately wanted to answer. I was pressing decline with my hands trembling. Not responding was challenging and had given me anxiety. I had to force myself to hit the red button every time a call came in. The emails went to a folder marked "later." According to his instruction, I couldn't even consider a response.

What was he saying here? I urged him to get to the point. "Guy, they can't use press that I have no control over. You told me I couldn't respond. I'm Mrs. Florida, of course there's a story here."

The justice system shouldn't rely on what's printed in the paper, especially when it's fake news. *Is that not the way it works?* Guy's normal confidence was clearly absent. He then told me that he needed to give me the worst-case scenario as my lawyer. *I should have trusted my gut. I should have gone balls to the wall and ignored his advice. I should have talked to the press and defended myself in public. I'm the media expert, the crisis manager.*

I didn't feel right about this impromptu legal meeting in any way, shape, or form. "Guy, I have been telling you from the beginning that she was cuddled up with the nursing home. They are in her ear and have the ear of the press. It's tainted opinions and a malicious agenda." I was up to my neck in dirt, standing in the swamp again. I walked out of the office in a fog that I couldn't see through. I couldn't wrap my head around this happening. I dropped my keys twice before I even got to my car.

I called my husband from the car and said, "It isn't good."

Unlike Guy and his poker face, he's been on the same page as me. He knew everything that I had been repeating for months and that my feelings were instinctual. My concerns and uncertainty in taking the deal were never a secret. "Evan, the prosecutor is making her decisions based on facts obtained by the nursing home," I said.

I was slightly annoyed by the conversation almost immediately; he shifted to talking about how he hates being strung up in the press himself and told me his ex-spouse is bound to make up stupid stories for attention as she has done before.

I'm annoyed by his focus on his issues. I understood that he has had things he wanted to address and explain, but in my eyes, they were insignificant nonsense. With what I was dealing with, they seemed even more insignificant.

I have made a serious effort to keep him out of the spotlight. *He should be thanking me. I have separated him as much as I can.* I attended the hearings without him and my family. There will be no one sitting in the gallery supporting me during sentencing. I would not subject them to the reporters and the negativity. *I can't do that to them. They didn't ask for the spotlight.*

In that moment, I realized that I signed up for this spotlight on the day that I won the title of Mrs. Florida.

"Hell hath no fury like a hustler with a literary agent."
—*Frank Sinatra*

Chapter 19 ———————

Back in Time

Here I was in another looming building with a picture on the wall that gave away the time. There was another metal detector and time warp of an office; there was another task, another meeting, another hurdle.

I felt violated that I was being tracked. They took a DNA sample, and I was being humiliated while peeing in a cup with someone watching. I had a sense of being watched, and knew that every time that I drove onto Palm Beach Island that my license plate was scanned and a federal officer got an email documenting my trips to Mar-a-Lago.

Carefully, they collected every detail about my life, categorizing and analyzing them. *I can't believe this is happening to me*, I thought, as I walked into the U.S. Probation Office. As I was on pre-trial supervision, I was a fingerprinted, documented, electronically-tracked U.S. citizen. They took my passport to prevent my flight out of the country. They probed about my appearances on RT International and questioned if I considered going to Russia for favorable extradition laws, as if I was going to try to escape charges for a misdemeanor of $17,000. This all seemed like some unnecessary, overreaching bullshit, at the very least. Their actions felt malicious, politically motivated, and overreaching.

"Well, I never thought I'd be here." I tried friendly conversation to lighten the mood, as I sat across from my newly appointed handler.

She seemed young, and I wondered what brought her into this line of work. Her office was packed with what I can assume was a small portion of a more extensive collection of superheroes, cartoon figurines, and plastic swords and shields. Odd-looking, costumed figurines lined her desk. Warlocks, Vikings, and a horse were carefully placed in formation.

No, maybe it's not a horse, it looks mythological. I glanced around at the decorated bookshelves lining the walls; the figurines seemed to glance back with judgment. Their little eyeballs were piercing; the inanimate colorful animals and humanoid objects were probably confused as to why I was there. *Maybe they are wondering as much as I am.* I imagined they sung "One of These Things" to mock me.

I wondered who her other clients were. *What am I to her? a client, a case, a number, a potential inmate? Maybe she's one of those people who goes to Comic-Con or other conferences dressed as her favorite characters. Perhaps she's a furry.* (You may know them as people who dress up in giant animal costumes.) *It's probably a cosplay thing.*

I entertained myself thinking about her going to a late-night fetish party in costume and felt better about humanizing this person, who probably didn't relate to me. I just wanted a clue to find some common ground between us.

She started to crack a smile—she did have a cute side smile. It wasn't much, but it was something. Maybe she entertained herself with thoughts of my almost waist-length, blonde hair, full makeup, and lashes. I was overdressed for the occasion, as usual. My oversized Tom Ford sunglasses were sitting on the edge of her desk, next to her costumed gang of characters. The stack of paper with my name on it made me uncomfortable. She went through every line item on the forms meticulously, asking me if I understood the terms after each. I wanted to get back to work; it all seemed so unproductive. My anxiety was building as I felt the hourglass getting tipped back over each time. It seemed it was finally running out.

"Do you have any questions?" she asked. I laughed a little. *My only questions are about your décor choices,* I thought.

"So, I call every Tuesday? What about travel? I need to go to Tampa next week for a meeting, and I have some things to do in Tallahassee. More importantly, I have a funeral for a family member," I said, panicking.

"Did you ask the judge for that?"

"I asked for travel for Washington, D.C. and New York City for work." *Those are my usual out-of-state spots.* "Can't I travel in Florida?" I asked.

"Not without specific permission. You can only go south to Miami and as far north as Vero," she responded.

Fuck, I think to myself. *Why didn't Guy mention this?* These restrictions are not going to work. I had a funeral to attend, and I was committed to being in Tallahassee. I was also supposed to help other families fight the backward-ass guardianship system. *Holy shit, they are stopping me from fighting back against the system.*

I knew Pam was going to be upset, and I hated making the call after I left the office. I had suffered another death, and but this time, I wouldn't be able to attend the funeral. I'm glad I met him before he died and got to know him a little. I didn't know how to tell her that I couldn't attend the funeral because I was a tracked citizen with minimal rights. I understood the magnitude of his death, and that she loved him very much. Her husband, best friend, and my birth father, Dale. They had reunited and married after so many years apart.

I scrolled for her contact, knowing that she would answer on the last ring. Even losing him won't slow her pace—she always kept moving.

I flashed back to the day she called me, eight years ago. It was a conversation that I never anticipated and a connection she thought was lost forever in the distant past.

I answered the phone, and she was crying. It wasn't an angry or sad cry—it was a happy deluge of emotion. "I just had lunch with him," she said. "Oh, my god Karyn, it's like no time has passed. I love him the same way I loved him forty years ago. I can't believe it. I reconnected with your birth father."

"WHHHHAAATTT?" This information was completely unexpected. "How the hell did this happen? Facebook?"

"I didn't know he was still here; he lives nearby. All this time, and he was here all along. I can't wait for you to meet him."

Dale was like I knew he would be—he was a patriot, a hunter, and a dedicated Army veteran, serving his country until he was physically unable. Dale's quiet demeanor was the opposite of Pam's fiery one. They moved in together, got married as quickly as they could, and made up for the lost time.

Before they reunited, I thought I looked like Pam, but I actually looked more like him. I had his longer face, his smile, and the shade of his blue eyes. Dale loved history and was a solid conservative. He was a freedom-loving, rifle-toting, flag-waving patriot.

The cherry on top was that my parents were so thrilled for them, and the connection was immediate between the four of them, just like it was with Pam and I when we first met.

Pam and Dale went down South to hang out with my parents and included them in their exciting engagement news. My dad glanced up from his iPad with Fox News babbling in the background as they entered. He was in his usual spot—the brown couch was worn into his shape. My mom wandered around the apartment with her aide in tow. She was wearing only one sock and looking everywhere for its mate.

The look on my dad's face was priceless as he stood up with his walker to salute his fellow veteran and shake his hand. They sat for hours talking history and war; it was beautiful to watch. Pam, meanwhile, and I took control to scout out the missing sock and put it on my mom's foot.

There was never any competition between them—my parents were still my parents. Some of my father's last words included him telling me how happy he was that even though we were losing him we had gained more family.

Pam had been a part of our lives for twenty years at that point. My parents and her parents got to know each other well. When my parents were younger, they took regular trips to Florida, and Pam was even in my bridal party at my first wedding. It was a questionable marriage that resulted in fantastic daughters.

Pam also had a track record of failed marriages, and there were a lot of similarities despite her twenty-year absence at the beginning of my life. She never liked my first husband. She put up with him and accepted my choice. In the end, she was right about him. Although my mom will always by my mom, when it came to motherly advice, Pam always nailed it.

I handed them my identification as I went through the security checkpoint for TSA, wondering if a notification would go off on the screen as I stood there. I wondered if she knows, but it was clear she doesn't. She handed me my identification as I proceeded through the security line, still feeling scrutinized, watched, and tracked. This was my regular morning flight—it got me into the city by 9:30 in the morning. I had a full day to get things done.

Walking through Newark has always been hectic; its energy is so different than West Palm Beach, where I began the day. People crowed together and moved forward in a mass towards the concourse. I donned my headphones and joined the march to the AirTran, where I punched the screen of a kiosk to get a train ticket to Penn Station.

I grabbed a seat and shoved my roll-along under my feet. We headed out of the light in New Jersey and into the darkness of New York, barreling through the tunnel into Penn Station. Gone were the graffiti-decorated cars of my youth—in 2019, the underground subways were much cleaner than they used to be.

The walk to my Park Avenue hotel from the train station was also part of my usual routine, but I was tired. I hailed a cab; sitting in traffic was slower than a walking pace. I made a conscious effort not to look at my phone—I knew the articles were hitting. I hit the "decline" button on my phone: I would give no interviews or explanations. I want to answer the questions and explain it all, but now was not the time.

It was only early fall, and I was cold and exhausted already. I wanted to hibernate. I studied the topic for my afternoon news program and hoped they didn't seen the headlines.

I am greeted with the usual friendly reception at the hotel, which has always been comforting, as I am a creature of habit. However, I realized how self-conscious I was becoming; I couldn't stop thinking that the front desk knew my story.

The big white bed in my room looked like exactly where I wanted to be. I laid down and stared at the gold and black chandelier wallpaper adorning one wall. The room had a nice walk-out balcony overlooking the roof of a shorter building below. Between the two green velvet chairs, the neat Scandinavian table held several books, including one by Bill Maher.

I thought about how I used to like him and hated that politics had us so divided. But his recent commentary seemed to be more logical. He, too, seemed to be waking up about the Democrat Party.

The topic for that day was the politics of division and how both parties are contributing to the divide. I would debate someone on the other side. I sat out on the balcony and made an espresso from the machine on the television stand to wake myself up. I called my second oldest, who lives in Manhattan and told her to come to the studio, and we would grab lunch and spend the afternoon together before she heads into work that evening.

Call waited beeped through as we talked. I felt a little panic rise up, but I brushed it off and told myself to be positive. I already knew it wasn't. I dreaded calling the producer back but knew I couldn't avoid it. "Karyn, can you be here early so we can talk?"

"Sure," I responded. "Do you want to talk now?"

There was a long pause, and I knew where it was heading. "We would prefer to do this in person. We saw the news," she said with a pause.

I figured getting right to the point was best, "What are you saying?"

Again, there was another pause. "We can't have you on."

I thought I was prepared, but I wasn't. I was exhausted, broken, battered, and the haters were getting what they wanted. There goes my career.

I realized that this was the beginning of more hurdles and more rejection. There was no solution, and there was nothing positive. I decided to crawl into the big, white bed. I just wanted to go back in time.

"We need more people speaking out. This country is not overrun with rebels and free thinkers. It's overrun with sheep and conformists."
—*Bill Maher*

Chapter 20

The Power of Love

My second oldest crawled into the big white bed in the hotel room. I wasn't sure if she heard the news in her New York City bubble, but she got right to it. "Mom, it's everywhere on social media—someone sent it to me this morning. If that's why you are laying here, you are stupid. The people who know you don't care."

She acted like her usual nonchalant self and glossed over the subject. "You can't lay here all afternoon. It isn't good for you. You know I like to sleep more than anyone."

"I don't know that I want to go to dinner with him. I'm just not up to it," I replied. The truth coming out of my mouth bothered me—after being let go from my news gig on a call and Googling myself, I felt beat down.

I thought about my clients and how—when they faced adversity—I gave them my "any press is good press" speech to minimize their emotional reactions. As I sat with my daughter, I tried to convince myself that this obstacle would pass; I wanted to limit my emotion but felt naked and exposed.

My daughter spoke, breaking my train of thought. "Mom, isn't this friend of yours some kind of a celebrity or something?" "Yes, something like that," I said. Her playing dumb was funny.

"He's familiar with tabloid articles, and I am sure this isn't a first," she replied. At her age, she rarely knows the people that I interview or my more famous friends—this made me smile a little.

"Mom, get ready, I'm hungry, and I have to go to work later." I looked at my missed calls, and he was one of them. I needed to get past the debilitating anxiety that was taking over and pulled myself together. I put my lashes on, straightened my hair, and grabbed my boots. Before we left, I walked into the large marble bathroom to see myself on the full-length mirror. I didn't look my best, but I didn't look bad either.

It was damp and cold—on our way out the doorman handed me a massive umbrella with the hotel logo emblazoned across it. There were no cabs to be seen, I attempted to call an Uber, but my daughter grabbed my arm. "Come on, mom, don't be such a princess. Let's hop on the subway and go downtown. Its rush hour and we'll probably get there quicker.

We walked the half block, ran down the stairs and scanned our MetroCards. The train was already on the platform and packed with straphangers. The subway trains are different but not so different from my childhood days of with my mom. Everyone is disconnected; no one even looks at each other. Each passenger has earbuds in or is absent in some other way.

As we exited the train a slightly hunched, older woman in a knit cap walked on. She carried plastic bags in both hands, an umbrella, and a tote bag. She looked like my mom. What if she wouldn't have had Alzheimer's? I pictured her riding the train and the buses into her eighties. Still would be a Brooklyn girl, moving quickly between the crowds of the city, with the pace of her age the only thing holding her back.

I stopped to watch the woman as the doors shut. This time, my daughter noticed and said with compassion. "Mom, we all watched you take care of her and how you struggled. The people around you know."

By the time we reached the street, the rain had stopped. The giant umbrella felt immediately cumbersome; it was more baggage than I needed. Like the weight of my thoughts, it was holding me down.

My nerves started to get to me. I wondered how I would explain everything. *Where will I begin this conversation? I haven't been able to talk about it at all to the press. The stories are all fake news.* Sharing this news over dinner with a friend who I respect now seemed overwhelming.

"He has a new album out. That's why he's in New York," I said to my daughter as we walk briskly towards West 16th Street.

"Oh, a bunch of new songs that I probably won't know either," she replied with a sarcastic smirk.

"You know his songs," I insisted.

"Yes, Mom. Yes, I do." She rolls her eyes a little. She's my eighties girl and she likes the music from that decade, but pretends a little, so she doesn't give me too much satisfaction.

As we walked, the first sentence of the article ran through my head: "Fresh from hosting a fund-raiser for the legal defense of Republican operative Roger Stone, conservative media commentator Karyn Turk on Friday admitted she stole her 83-year-old mother's Social Security checks." It was an aggravating, inaccurate account of what happened. I thought about the old lady we just saw in the subway and how, if she knew about the article, she'd be clutching her purse as I walked by.

The door opened with a gust of wind. I immediately spotted Huey's familiar smile, and suddenly I don't care about the press. Huey and I disagree on politics, but it doesn't matter. I'm sure he's delighted that my daughter is on the opposite end of things and gives me a hard time about current events. I knew they'd hit it off, and they did.

Huey Lewis is recognizable, but at this restaurant, he was just another patron. We sat at a prominent table, and no one stopped him for an autograph or photo. Huey once told me that his love for music was why he was on stage. He never thought of himself as famous, even though he knew he was. He's always been laid back, humble and charming.

My thoughts ran as I gulped my pinot grigio. I didn't know how to approach this—my head was really out of the game. I thought about him in concert in 1984 when Huey Lewis and the News opened for .38 Special. His music was the soundtrack to my teenage years. I wished I could go back in time—I wanted the opportunity to rewrite history and things for the better.

My mind drifted to a movie soundtrack that Huey's songs dominated, *Back to the Future,* which bared a resemblance to how I was feeling. In the movie, Marty McFly fears that he will become like his parents, despite his ambitions. His father, George, is a coward being bullied by Biff, his supervisor at work. His mother, Lorraine, is unhappy, overweight, and an alcoholic. They met when Lorraine's father hit George with his car. He brought George in the house to recover, and she nursed him back to health.

Marty is independent and has an eccentric friend, a mad scientist named Doc. True to the decade, they meet in a mall parking lot after closing so Doc can show Marty his latest invention—a stainless-steel, DeLorean built, nuclear-powered time machine. It turns out Doc obtained the plutonium to power the car from Libyan terrorists, who showed up at the mall to kill the duo.

During the frenzy, Marty activates the time machine and is accidentally transported to 1955 where he encounters a teenage George and discovers that Biff was bullying him even in high school. Marty finds Doc in 1955, and Doc instructs him not to leave his house or interact with anyone, as he could inadvertently alter the future. Their only option to get Marty back to the present day is by harnessing electricity from a lightning strike to power the time machine.

Marty, however, has already interacted with people; he has prevented his parents from meeting by saving George from the car accident and changed the outcome of the future. Now Marty has to make his parents fall in love or face being erased from existence.

Marty's mother is now enamored with him instead of George. He devises a plan to bring his parents together at the school dance, but before he can carry it out, Biff's gang stuffs Marty in the trunk of the car. As Biff is about to assault Lorraine, cowardly George steps in, unexpectedly grows a pair, and punches Biff, knocking him out. When the lightning strike sends Marty back to 1985, he realizes that the change of events in 1955 has led to changes in the present day. His father is a self-confident, successful author, and his mother is fit and happy. Biff is a now reserved personality working as a valet.

If only it were that easy to go back in time and change fate. Maybe I could go back to stop Alzheimer's, but even if I couldn't do that, I could still change my mistakes. I could make the decision not to admit her into the horrible, neglectful nursing home. If I never put her there, then there would have been no bill to fight over. I could have avoided the litigious, swamp-dwelling lawyers. There would be no guardian. She wouldn't have suffered with bedsores. Maybe she'd still be here, and she'd still be singing. Perhaps she would even remember me.

I was glad when my daughter excused herself for a few minutes, leaving me to address the elephant in the room. It takes Huey less than a second. "What's wrong?" he quietly asked me.

I gulped my wine. "You don't know?"

"Know what?"

"It's all over the internet," I replied.

"You know I don't do the social media thing like you." His statement was true. Huey has always been old school; he lives on a ranch in Montana, hunting and fishing. He was only in New York to promote his new album.

"It's hard even to know where to begin," I said. I tried to explain the story in simple terms. I tried not to sound like a conspiracy theorist, as I told him about the horrific way she died, the plea deal, the media, and the outcome.

By this time my daughter, back in her chair, has thoughtfully grabbed me another glass of wine. "Here mom," she said, sliding it over. "I keep telling her not to read it, that her friends don't care what the paper says."

"I agree," Huey replied. He looked at me and said, "You have a brilliant daughter. She's like you." His calmness was just what I needed, and I realized they do support me. I felt safe. The dinner continued with a weight lifted and an invitation.

"You should get away and visit the ranch," Huey said. "Shut off the internet. Just stop all of it."

I didn't know how to tell him that this was impossible—I couldn't go anywhere without permission or travel without being tracked. I laughed a little to myself about how I would explain to my probation officer in her Comic-Con decorated office that there was a valid work purpose for me to relax on Huey Lewis's ranch.

"It's true. I do like cheering people up."
—*Huey Lewis*

Chapter 21

Judgment Without Knowledge

I was so consumed with my crisis, I forgot to get a ticket for the jitney to the Hamptons and was trying to come with a plan B. I ran around with a rolling suitcase in tow and my earbuds in, ignoring everyone around me. I headed underground onto the subway, emerging into Grand Central and was surrounded by its massive concourse, tile accents, and nostalgic details. It is one of my favorite places in the city; it holds an energy that's special and historic.

I was heading to the furthest reaches of Long Island to the North Fork TV Festival, and it looked like the word hasn't reached these far-off places. My interviews for *Behind the Headlines* were still on target. If word has reached them, there has been no call or cancellation.

I was wracked with anxiety, but there weren't many options. I have waited months for these interviews; this was a bucket list experience. *They may shun me on the red carpet. Who knows?* I got last seat on the jitney, which had to be a good sign. I found a seat next to an older woman who looked like she had fully shopped for the trip—her food items burst out of several bags on the floor below. I needed to decompress and didn't want anyone to talk to me, so I put in my earbuds and fired up my iPad to begin researching the television shows highlighted at the event and review the itinerary.

I have emails, but Guy's voice echoed in my head: "No interviews, no explanations until sentencing." I dropped them into a folder to address them later, but there was one I couldn't ignore. It was a tip from a journalist I worked with pretty regularly, who gave me a heads up that a tabloid has been poking around, possibly compensating some people who were estranged from me, like my ex-husband and his ex-spouse.

"Shit! Really?" I said out loud. The headphones threw me off and I apologized to the grocery lady next to me.

I knew it was a matter of time—his ex was just miserable and relished playing the victim. I have only had one somewhat memorable conversation with my ex in fifteen years; it was memorable only because I remembered why we didn't speak. He was a Hillary supporter, who moved on to Bernie.

I already knew the deal—both of them were still twisted in the past somewhere.

My ex had nothing new to say. His stories were twenty years old, and he has distorted them over time until only a grain of truth remained. They were things he thought I would be ashamed of, and I wondered if they would even cover them.

Before the millennium, things were pretty good in New York City. I had missed the dawn of disco at Studio 54, which had always been my real dream, but there was a new dawn of nightlife in the 1990s—upscale gentleman's clubs. If I was going to make a better life for myself and get away from an awful marriage, I needed to sock away as much as possible in a short period of time. Bartending and cocktail waitressing at Scores afforded that opportunity. It was truly the hottest club in New York City—every night was like a red carpet with a celebrity lineup.

The Italian club managers treated me really well. I wasn't dancer material, with my skinny, boyish frame. My ability to work behind the bar and back up the managers and VIP clients made up for my falling flat in other areas, pun intended.

I had also worked at Hooters during college when my oldest daughter was little. Again, I made up for what I lacked in the hooter department by being the most enthusiastic waitress in the restaurant. I always picked up shifts and worked promotions. I'd even hula hoop in front of the restaurant, which sat at the entrance of Universal Studios.

I also worked off-site at golf outings in Hooters' cute white shorts outfit. I drove a golf cart, delivering beverages to CEOs and influential people on the course. The Hooters girls would hang out with the Orlando Magic players; we even attended a party or two at Shaquille O'Neil's house. At the restaurant, we would take Polaroids with tourists, and I would sign my name with a little heart. It was a job mixed with a party. It was appealing and fun.

The environment at the gentleman's club in Manhattan was even better than I expected. I had heard stories; there was a shooting, and the management had mafia connections. All I experienced was a fun place to work. It was a cool place with great music that gave an opportunity to meet interesting people. There were plenty of A-listers at Scores. Howard Stern was a regular; there were New York Yankees, rappers, producers, and I was the cute blonde providing alcohol in a bustier. I was a part of the in-crowd, but the dollar signs adding up in the bank meant it was temporary. A new life was calling me.

I imagined the tabloid meeting with my ex and him telling the reporters these ancient stories, with his own twist, and I forgot about my present story for a minute. The old memories were more pleasant; I wished I was a young cocktail waitress at a strip club, which was better than being strung up like a criminal who steals from old ladies.

I ignored the phone calls coming from the people who wanted to be nosey; they were fakes and women who wanted to see me fail. I reminded myself that I was glad to escape to the Hamptons.

Once off the jitney, everyone dispersed in different directions. The ferry was parked at the dock, and I dragged my suitcase over the bumpy parking lot toward it. I definitely needed coffee and was happy to see a coffee shop attached to the hotel on the corner.

Before I could grab the handle, the door opened, and Dr. Frasier Crane appeared. I was a little starstruck by this fellow conservative and Hollywood icon, but I was even more struck by the irony of struggling with my internal crisis. Here was America's favorite therapist who is opening the door—how apropos.

"Thank you," I smiled wide, pushing up my cheeks. "Thank you," he says in his very recognizable, deep voice. I blurted, "You have no idea how much I need therapy, just having you open the door here is helpful."

He smiled and laughed. "So glad I could help," he said. I am obviously in the right place, I thought. My panic subsided. For the time being, I was able to forget my problems and focused on going *Behind the Headlines* with the celebrities at the festival. The hustle began as we followed the itinerary around the different venues. I was lost in the pleasant pace of being busy, and there were great restaurants, beautiful sights, and screenings to look forward to. I shut the notifications off on my phone and figured that posting was probably a better idea after I left. I didn't need the comments on my posts to tip-off anyone here that I was a criminal.

The day executed pretty flawlessly, and it got better when the screenings began. The red carpet was crowded. The flash-bulbs popped, the cameras rolled, the hosts lined up with their microphones in hand. One after another, the interviews began.

My last interview was the best. As Kelsey Grammer approached, he gave me advice. My red-carpet therapist left me with a moment and a phrase that will carry me through the storm that's just begun to hit.

"Judgment without knowledge is the greatest of all crimes, and there's a lot of no knowledge running around right now."
—Kelsey Grammer

Chapter 22 ————————

Welcome to the Fishbowl

𝕬s we came into the terminal in Palm Beach, the reality hit me like a sledgehammer—the place that I couldn't wait to escape to is not at all where I wanted to be in the present moment. My head hurt, and I was exhausted; the New York City adrenaline rush has definitely worn off. As I trudged for the parking garage, the familiar warmth and humidity greeted me. The palm trees greeted me, waving with a light breeze as I headed out on I-95 South to get back to my actual life, and not the fantasy land that I escaped to.

The next week would be a barrage of questions from friends, some genuine, many not. It's eye-opening when you see how quickly you weed out real friends from the others—my husband's gut instincts usually trump mine in this regard.

We were back in our usual routine, but I got up unusually early. "You should go back to bed," my husband said.

I didn't sleep much. I was going to mention it but was surprised that he hadn't noticed.

"Today's the big day," I replied.

He remembered; his memory is better at this than mine. Remembering his daily schedule is sometimes a struggle; his feelings are hurt if I don't listen to him and remember his lunch appointments or new client dinners.

"Yes, it is," he said.

This was the day I had waited for. It was a day I knew that we would uncover details; a day that Ron Denman so smartly suggested. We would depose the guardian, the nursing home director, and the attorneys. I already knew a lot and anticipated there was much more to uncover. *Fucking monsters,* I thought. It was just all so unbelievable.

I had no idea just how unbelievable things were about to become.

The glass conference room was visible as I approached the lobby. It was a fishbowl of a conference room, similar to the one we had at CBS Radio during my days behind the scenes as their marketing director.

My lawyer, Ron Denman's young associate, Grant, was seated at the table. He made eye contact, and I noticed the backs of two people and the court reporter at the end of the table. It was Amy, the guardian, and none other than O'Connell. I inhaled deeply, trying to calm myself as I opened the door.

Grant was composed. I hadn't met him yet, but he sounded like Ron in his delivery. "Let's take a few minutes in the other room before we begin," he said.

I followed him to another conference room on the other side of the lobby, and he shut the door. "I know this is emotional for you, but if you are going to sit in, you can't show them that. Just don't comment—stay disconnected and don't make eye contact if you can help it. The good news is the other side didn't prepare this guardian well. She came in with accordion files and had an arm full of folders stacked with papers. There are tons of paperwork and emails—I would imagine there's a lot in there to uncover," he said. This time, the paper stacks weren't making me uncomfortable.

The day my mother died the guardian tried to show up. She called the funeral home, as if she was handling my mother's last wishes and arrangements. I could only assume this was an attempt to hide the abuse.

I was finally a step ahead in the game. I had been discovered that the guardianship ends at death in Florida, and there was no way she was getting anywhere near my mother now. How could she not have known about the nine bedsores eating at my mother's flesh? Her bones were exposed. How did she not see the bruises on her face? Why wouldn't she respond? Did she ever even visit? Will we ever get answers?

Back in the conference room, I got up to make coffee. I may not acknowledge them, but my piddling around behind them had to be uncomfortable. For the second time, I felt like there was controlled chaos and things were not as bad as the criminal case makes them seem. Ron and Grant had a plan.

I sat back down with my coffee. I wrote emails on my phone and worked while he slowly began his questioning. O'Connell objected again and again, with "attorney-client privilege" as his go-to.

He represented both the guardian and the nursing home—how was this not a conflict? There was a $16.4 million judgment for "doing a family wrong in guardianship" and they were still operating in this manner.

Nothing had changed. *Oh, that's right, I'm in the swamp. Logic doesn't apply here.* The swamp is bizarro world where actions don't matter, politics on the left is dirty, and people manipulate facts, pepper in untruths, and do anything to discredit someone to shut them up.

The resistance is real, not just a Facebook hashtag from women in pink-knitted caps. It is the inability of the other side to come to terms with a difference of opinion to compensate for their lack of control by acting like a sick little mafia.

The world in the conference room was just like the world outside of it—divisive and the opposite of how America is supposed to be. The left pulled the strings of the DOJ, and the FBI. This is bigger than what was happening to me in this glass fishbowl.

Amy's depo continued—she squirmed a little as I glanced up from my screen. She knew so little about my mom. The guardianship system is such a facade.

I felt her anxiety from across the table; her aura had taken a shift to angry, nervous energy. Grant's questions were great. As O'Connell tried to stop her from answering, there was a smugness that I began to see between them. She did it, she's proud of it, and she was clearly excited to pass over the papers.

O'Connell was almost smirking. It became clear that she reported me, and they directed her to do so. It was all there in black and white, documented for law enforcement and the government to see. *How is this possible? How can this be?*

Grant began to really probe her; he called her out on her lack of evidence for the claims she made. I felt my skin getting hot, as I stared into the void that is her soul.

"Tell her to stop staring at me!" she screamed.

The court reporter was taken back. Grant was thrown off. I went back to my phone, as Granted turned to me asked if I was intentionally looking at her.

I explain that I must have zoned out for a minute and didn't realize what had happened. I promised to be more conscious. I certainly didn't want to look again.

I was just as shaken by her lack of emotion as she appeared to be about Grant's questions. As the hours rolled by, I realized that I was up against something really extreme. I was so deep there is no going back; there was no simple way out of the quicksand they had placed around me.

The executive director's deposition was equally compelling, with plenty of inaccuracies. I had researched the facility—it had a one-star ACHA rating and questionable inspection reports.

I knew about another unlawful death lawsuit, swept under the rug and settled out of court. A family had waged a lawsuit over an infection in a man's penis that led to sepsis. His daughter's plight sounded familiar and followed the same pattern of horrific neglect.

I was not sure if leaving older adults to die with their flesh being eaten and riddled with infections was murder. It seemed like murder to me, and I stared it in the face. It was the bearded man reincarnated. Her perception was spot on, but her warnings went unheeded. I comforted her blurry thoughts masked by dementia, and I will likely never forgive myself for the level of naivety I had; it was just like avoiding the robbers on the subway, running through the cars looking for an angel to help me. I had found two so far—one was still issuing probing questions at the bearded man, and the other was back in his office in Tampa. *When this is all over, I should buy Ron and Grant red berets and white tee shirts with all-seeing eyes. They can wear them to court.* I distracted myself with these random thoughts to stop myself from wanting to crawl over the conference table and rip both their nuts off.

As I sat there, I realized that it was only the beginning, and the storm was still brewing. The sunshine peeped through the clouds before disappearing again as the stormy air started circulating, just like it did out west over the Everglades. An unstoppable thunderstorm was approaching, and I needed to avoid getting struck by the lighting, but I felt like I was standing at the Trump International Golf Course holding up a metal driver toward the sky.

"You've got to show the world who you are before it tells you. Otherwise, you become victim to someone you're not."
—Chris Colfer, Struck By Lightning

Chapter 23 ————————

A Sentence Harsher
Than Epstein's

eing an only child has taught me to survive when the circumstances call for me to stand alone. There was no way
I was going to subject my children and my husband to my sentencing hearing. I would not have them strung up in the press.
There was reason to have them exposed in the back of the room.
I had been advised that I should bring them to soften my edge
and look more relatable to the judge, but I weighed the pros
and cons and decided that I couldn't risk them being dragged
through the swamp.

It was another Florida day that looked like so many others.
The sun was out, and the palm trees swayed along the side of
the road as I drove alone to the courthouse. I thought about
how normal this day was for everyone else on the highway and
how desperately alone I was in this fight. I didn't even touch the
radio; I just drove in silence. I was already in mourning. I knew

that today would be another death—the death of justice and my innocence in believing there was an unbiased legal process.

I was questioning everything. *Why the hell didn't I ask Ron Denman to come here? He understands this dynamic so much more than Guy and David.* I knew this was a mistake. I should have pushed for him to be here. I started a mantra to myself about leaving the past in the past. *There were no do-overs—you did the best you could in the moment with the information you had. That's the best you could have done.* The pep talk was not very comforting, but it was better than becoming hysterical and losing my cool entirely.

The nursing home was sure to create a spectacle. The bearded man had been plotting for weeks, calling in a posse of haters from my past to join him for the main event. I knew it, and I shrugged it off. The amount of energy he seemed to be expending on this passive aggressiveness was a sure shot of desperation. I had bigger things to deal with—I was fighting for my freedom. This was the last and final moment before it could be stolen, just like they stole our freedom with the guardianship.

I arrived in the parking lot across the street looking for the black Porsche where he would be waiting. I was alone, but I needed a little protection. I didn't feel like being caught in an ambush as I walked in. He stepped out of the car to greet me and offered an understanding but awkward sideways hug. "I need a few minutes," I told him.

We watched as the crowd began to build outside the doors of the federal courthouse. I spotted the nursing home posse joined by O'Connell. There were several journalists and a woman who resembled the prosecutor.

I texted my lawyers. They were dwarfed by the doorway crowd and were waiting off to the side. "There is no way I'm walking over," I told Guy via text.

He responded quickly. "Relax they will walk in before us. We will follow. You just wait where you are. Let the press think you already went in. Wait till we are all inside and give it ten minutes. They won't start without you." That last part was the best part of the whole text; he was right, they couldn't start without me. They couldn't feed me to the lions if I wasn't there. I stood in the parking lot trying to remain incognito, while my bodyguard leaned on his car. Time was passing too quickly, and I couldn't avoid it much longer.

"Let's go" I said, and he walked by my side across the street and past the line of journalists that I consciously ignored.

The metal detector greeted us beyond the doorway. The elevator ascended and we arrived at our destination. The large metal doors opened to the sound of screaming. The three-ring circus had begun with a side show act.

David was yelling at the ring master. The prosecutor was in an appropriate circus costume—it was a bright purple suit, the color of Barney the dinosaur, and hung baggily off her frail frame.

I knew what was happening; she was going back on the deal. It was THAT deal—the one that prosecutors don't go back on, the one that I had been assured that if they did the whole system would crumble.

I understood this old woman had nothing to lose. She had dozed off at the pre-sentencing hearing, only to be re-awakened by a staff member as the judge asked her a question. She had to be approaching eighty, or she at least looked it. So, what did it matter if she went off the rails on this case? She would just retire after it was over. She would grab her pension and run. She was a typical litigation attorney.

I was all too familiar with everything now. I had learned the game.

I entered the courtroom, making eye contact only with my bodyguard. He sat down in the only empty section of the gallery next to *The Palm Beach Post* reporter. I watched him start to chat with her; she seemed to be consciously ignoring him, mirroring my behavior as I walked past the reporters on my way into the courthouse.

The lawyers flanked me—Guy was on the right, and David was on the left. They shielded me from view of the packed gallery on the prosecution's side. I could feel the bearded man—I didn't even need to look. His actors surrounded him in the gallery.

The side show act was over, and it was time for the main event. The three-ring circus was led by the small, frail, costume-clad ringmaster. She resembled more of an emcee than a lawyer adhering to an ethical standard of practice.

I prayed hard that Guy and David were prepared. Guy knew the magistrate, Bruce Reinhart, very well; they had worked on the Jeffrey Epstein case together. It should have been a positive connection, but it was becoming clear that his connection to that case, in light of the recent suicide of Jeffrey Epstein, was likely going to be more of a curse than a blessing. In the days before my sentencing, the newspapers were digging deep into the old facts of the Jeffrey Epstein case and the legal players that surrounded it. Those players were on my side in the courtroom and against me on the bench.

I had hired the "high profile" law firm for good reason—their perceived connections and ability to make things happen. Guy was the same lawyer who received that secret plea deal for

Jeffery Epstein to avoid a Grand Jury hearing. The 2006 agreement would have swept the case under the rug. The deal, issued in a letter from the assistant state attorney and addressed to Guy was uncovered by the team compiling the book, *Epstein: Dead Men Tell No Tales*. It clearly illustrated just what a sweet deal it could have been for the Democrat-tied, billionaire sex offender. The letter read:

> "By this letter, I am confirming the offer of settlement to your client, Jeffrey Epstein. Should you accept this settlement, the state will not proceed with Grand Jury proceedings tomorrow. Plea to Aggravated Assault with the Intent to Commit a Felony, a third-degree felony. Adjudication will be withheld, and your client will be placed on 5-year probation. There was the need for a psycho-sexual evaluation and successful completion of any recommended treatment. He would need to fully pay back the costs of the investigation by the Palm Beach Police Department. He could even apply for early termination of probation after three years if there were no violations and all conditions have been successfully completed."

Guy made that happen; it was even sweeter than the final deal Jeffrey Epstein accepted.

I thought that someone capable of this feat would be a legal magician and based on his history, a misdemeanor plea deal for a Social Security fraud charge should have been easy, especially when you factor in that this was money that my parents had paid into the system. It was money that my mother capably made me fiduciary of. I was intrigued that the government treated this as their money because Social Security is a program that private citizens work for and pay into.

Reinhart was in his robe, playing the only role that I knew him in as the magistrate for my case. His relationship in representing Jeffrey Epstein's employees so many years ago was not something I was thinking about as I awaited my fate.

A little while before my sentencing, it was clear that this whole relationship between Reinhart and Guy might not have been a chess move I should have taken. Over a decade earlier, *The Miami Herald* broke the story: "Deflecting blame, Acosta pointed finger at others. Why they may have some explaining to do." The article stated:

> "On Oct 23, 2007, as federal prosecutors in South Florida were in the midst of tense negotiations to finalize a plea deal with accused sex trafficker Jeffrey Epstein, a senior prosecutor in their office was quietly laying out plans to leave the U.S. attorney's office after 11 years. On that date, as emails were flying between Epstein's lawyers and federal prosecutors, Bruce E. Reinhart, now a federal magistrate, opened a limited liability company in Florida that established what would become his new criminal defense practice."

Then there was a 2011 affidavit, where Reinhart swore, under penalty of perjury that "he was not part of the team involved in Jeffrey Epstein's investigation and therefore was not privy to any confidential information about the case" while he was at the U.S. Attorney's Office. However, as *The Miami Herald* pointed out:

> "Reinhart's former supervisors in the U.S. Attorney's Office filed a court paper contradicting him, saying that while Bruce E. Reinhart was an assistant U.S. attorney, he learned confidential, non-public information about the Epstein matter."

As Julie K. Brown of *The Miami Herald* wrote in 2019:

> "Reinhart's defection was one of many highly unusual turns that the [Jeffrey] Epstein case took 12 years ago, moves that could merit examination as the multimillionaire's controversial non-prosecution agreement is dissected in the wake of his arrest last week on sex trafficking charges."

In 2015, Reinhart defended Jeffrey Epstein on Newsmax, not as his attorney of seven years, but as a legal expert and a former U.S. prosecutor. He was back on the bench when he was appointed as a U.S. magistrate, nearly a year after R. Alexander Acosta began his stint as labor secretary.

Acosta resigned on July 19, 2019 over his handling of the Jeffrey Epstein case. *The Palm Beach Post* recorded Reinhart as saying, "It's been a good week in our house."

Now I was in his house at his mercy and realized he had a sorted and murky history. I hadn't considered that I was a female Republican and Trump supporter, and Jeffery Epstein was a

Democrat sex offender. It's pretty sick and twisted—not just what Jeffrey Epstein did, but the backwards ass legal system. Who does it favor anyway? Top off the Epstein connections with him "committing suicide" (wink-wink) barely 4 weeks before my court hearing.

Guy's calm demeanor was concerning but my faith in David's aggression made up for my slightly uneasy feelings. It made sense to bring a bodyguard. I needed someone to have my back if the press swarmed, or if the legal evil invaded my personal space.

I whispered and nudged Guy trying to gauge his lack of reaction. He seemed to think silence on his behalf was somehow strategic. However, David's passion was evident as he loudly advocated for me from the podium.

The purple suit finally grabbed her chance with the microphone, "We just wanted to say, although this is a misdemeanor offense, that it is quite a serious offense, in that it involves the backdrop to the false statement." I held back the eye roll that I wanted to express. It always seems to come down to a "false statement." This must be in the first chapter of the prosecutorial manual. Find a "false statement," then attack with vengeance.

Her passion was a match for the inaccuracies that she told the magistrate. *There's one—no, there are two.* I kept counting as she ranted. *Holy shit, there's five and six!* It was like she had taken the information during pillow talk with the bearded man and was now presenting it to the court with no consideration for the accuracy of her statements. This witch-hunt had me burning at the stake in the courtroom.

The magistrate asked me if I wanted to speak. I did, I had to. I knew it wasn't going to help the outcome, but I might have at least had a measure of control with the articles that would be printed. They might quote something I said on my own behalf. They had before—it was worth a shot.

As the magistrate began to close the hearing, his monologue began:

> "The history and characteristics of defendant are admirable. I read all of the letters. I credit all of them. I believe Ms. Turk has done a lot of good in her life and continues to do a lot of good in her life. She clearly loves her family. She clearly tried to do her best to be a positive force here in society."

For a moment my ears perked up, but it was only a second before the tirade went south:

> "I will note it is admirable that she has come today with a restitution check, so I gave her some credit for that, but that's not the be all and end all. We cannot have the appearance in the American criminal justice system that you can buy your way out of jail and that you can just come to court with money, if you have money, and that somehow washes away what happened here. So, while I give her credit for the fact that she is prepared to pay full restitution, I don't give a tremendous amount of weight because that's simply a factor of her financial well-being."

Huh, I thought, *that seems like bias.* Then he went on:

> "And as I said, we can't have the appearance that you can buy your way out of prison. In terms of

the other effects that counsel talked about on
Mrs. Turk and her life and reputation and all
of that, choices in life have consequences, I'm
sorry to tell you. So again, while I acknowledge
those and perhaps, they are a component of the
punishment that Ms. Turk will suffer for the rest
of her life as a result of this crime, they, in and
of themselves, are not sufficient in my view to
achieve the goals of sentencing as required under
the sentencing statute."

Then he said the words I wasn't prepared for:

"I am going to impose a term of incarceration
in this case."

He went on to say:

"We often talk in the criminal justice system
about how a sentence needs to send a message.
I can't tell you how many times I've stood in
courtrooms like this one and, in fact, [I've stood
in] this one as a lawyer and heard a judge say,
'Well, we need to send a message,' and I looked
around and there was nobody to hear it. Well,
in your case, they are going hear the message
because you're a public figure. So, in terms of
the need to send deterrence to others, again, the
sentence in this case needs to send a message,
and the message needs to be [that] you don't
get to steal from the government of the United

States and not go to jail. So, that is the message I am sending. It is the judgment of the court that the defendant, Karyn Turk, is committed to the Bureau of Prisons to be imprisoned for one month."

Prison. I am going to prison. It sunk in as I looked at Guy. I couldn't read his emotion. David was visibly shocked. The gallery and the cast lead by the bearded man and purple suit burst out in a standing ovation. My bodyguard sat with his jaw dropped and his chin on the floor.

Then, there was the matter of the prison he was designating me to. There would be no minimum-security, federal camp for my white-collar misdemeanor. No Club Fed. I was to be housed in the Federal Detention Center in downtown Miami. It was a maximum security prison with everyone from pre-trial inmates to gang members, drug dealers, and murderers.

It was nonsensical. My sentence was harsher than the initial deal that they offered Jeffery Epstein.

I sat silently and waited for everyone to leave the courtroom. The was nothing to say. There was no one I was going to address. I gave it enough time to let the evil disperse into the street outside. I said, "What the fuck just happened? Why didn't you point out the inaccuracies? She lied! Why didn't you say anything, Guy? I'm so confused. How can they send a message because of my job as a conservative commentator?" David was quick to reassure me. "We know how you are feeling, I'll file your appeal right away."

I was under the impression that an appeal meant there would be a motion to stay. Just like most people, you may assume an appeal means you don't serve the imposed sentence until the appeal is heard. You already know I was in prison and conservative commentators and outspoken Republicans are certainly not everyone else in today's divided America.

The days after my sentencing were filled with interviews. I didn't stop. It was time to fight back. I was done pressing the red button and sending the calls to voicemail; it was time to face the situation head on.

I knew that's what my parents would want. They would want me to fight for justice and fairness in the country that they worked so hard to be a part of. It's the land of the free and home of the brave—it is America that I still love, despite being thrown on the tracks in front of an oncoming train. I believe in the power of freedom and that good eventually prevails over evil.

"Every story has an end, but every ending is a beginning."
—*Karyn Turk*

Epilogue

𝔄s I sit here today, it's over a year since I finished writing this book. I struggle with signing the settlement agreement with the nursing home. After what we were put through, part of me wants closure, and part of me wants vindication. Should I move forward with a jury trial and subject my family to a long, painful trial or put this to rest? How do I focus on turning the tables to create a legacy that honors my mother's memory? The formation of a 501(c)(3) called Guardian Watchdogs is a start—an organization that backs up families through private investigations. These investigations can support their legal battles and assist the media with background for stories. The stories aren't just families' opinions. We will assemble credible facts, surveillance, and evidence to back up their claims. Helping the vulnerable have a voice when the powers that are too corrupt take a stand for the people they should be protecting.

In a strange twist that virtually no one saw coming, Joe Biden is occupying the White House. Curtis Sliwa—the founder of the Guardian Angels who was such an inspiration in my childhood—is currently running for mayor of New York City. The things I wrote here from my heart so many months ago have more relevance than ever. Historical recurrence is happening in such a profound way. We cannot help but see the similarities between Joe Biden to Jimmy Carter. Gas lines and crime waves bring all of us back in time to 1979. Israel is in turmoil, and I think about my parent's story of escape from Austria and the Nazis more than ever. The slippery slope of socialism is hard to ignore. Reverting to look forward is something we should all do more often. Radicals are looking to erase our history, giving us no way to formulate a proper perspective. Historic reflection gives us data to predict possible outcomes of choices that we may make as a society.

What's happened to me since I was released from prison? So much. The prison experience was something that will forever have an impact on my life. The way I approach my journey and the way I judge others and their choices has dramatically changed. The women that I met in those thirty days deserve their stories to be heard. To be acknowledged and understood is something that we all need. Their mistakes do not define them as people. That is my next manuscript, what I am writing now. My next book is for them.

I have gotten back to a sense of normality; I have been blessed that my "canceling" seems to be temporary, and the real friends and people who care about me have stuck by my side. I am very thankful for all of them. I am filling in as a guest host on Real America's Voice, reporting on politics and news. I have an iHeartRadio show that goes "behind the headlines" each week on topics the mainstream media isn't covering or are misconstruing. I have a weekly column in the published reporter where I contribute opinions on everything from the daily news headlines to personally impactful topics. I have some crisis management projects and appear as a media commentator every chance I can. I am back to traveling without being tracked by the government like an animal. I have spent more time helping candidates that I believe in. I was blessed before this crazy experience and after. I don't forget that, ever. Not for a second.

The people that turned their backs in my crisis are also not forgotten. The haters that relished in my struggle are some of my biggest motivators. Thank you for being the bottom-feeding as*holes that you are. You have taught me so much about life and given me numerous opportunities through your blogging, tweets, and rants about me being a horrible person. You are perfect as you are, don't change a thing.

Where do I go from here? I'm not sure, but I am enjoying the ride. I was asked on a podcast today, "What's your biggest takeaway for people hearing the story and listening to this show?" My answer was, "Live your truth and live without fear."

A special thank you to everyone that has helped me complete this book and has listened to my constant questions of whether it's good enough to share with the world. I love you for believing in me.